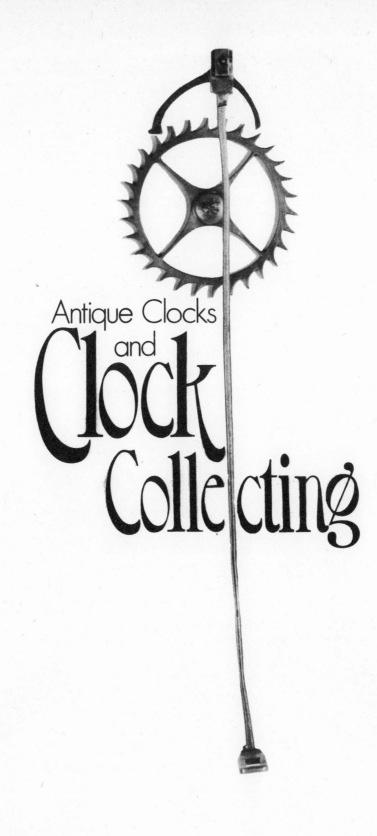

Antique Clocks
and
Clock
Collecting

Antique Clocks
and
Clock
Collecting

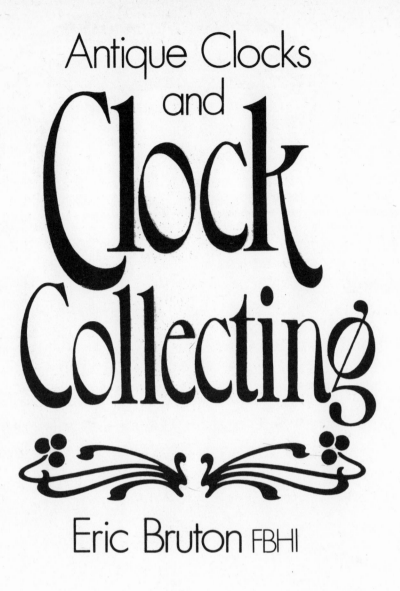

Eric Bruton FBHI

Hamlyn

London · New York · Sydney · Toronto

Published by
The Hamlyn Publishing Group Limited
London · New York · Sydney · Toronto
Astronaut House, Feltham, Middlesex, England

© Copyright The Hamlyn Publishing Group Limited 1974

ISBN 0 600 31795 1

Phototypeset in England by Filmtype Services Limited
Printed in Czechoslovakia

1 *half-title page* An early anchor escapement used by Thomas Tompion after 1675. The curved anchor at the top soon became more symmetrical and flatter.

2 *frontispiece* Dial of a clock by Tompion & Banger, with calendar, strike and chime, and a mock pendulum.

3 *right* Front plate of a chiming clock by Gretton. The striking is controlled by snail and rack. Fitzwilliam Museum, Cambridge.

Contents

Why and what to collect   6

Where to find, and find out about, clocks   12

The early period: Before the pendulum   20

The middle period: The pendulum in England   32

The middle period: The pendulum in Holland, France, Germany and the United States   58

The later period: Novelty, special and early factory clocks   80

Postscript: Taking a clock home   88

Bibliography   94

Index   95

Acknowledgments   96

Why and what to collect

4 Probably the most famous of all
reproductions, the astronomical clock made
from Giovanni de Dondi's original
instructions written in about 1364. The
long-established clockmakers, Thwaites & Reed,
of Clerkenwell, London, have made five
of these big clocks so far. They make
reproductions of other famous clocks, too.

It would be difficult to isolate the historical moment when someone acquired a clock as a curiosity rather than as a timekeeper – when he 'collected' it. In the 16th and 17th centuries, a domestic clock could well have been the most valuable article possessed by a household. It would have been treasured and willed down through the family for generations. Thus, when clock-owning families united through marriage, there would be a marriage of clocks as well, which would be treasured as heirlooms and form the nucleus of a 'collection' in the same way as the family silver.

Clocks were described by the two 17th-century diarists, Pepys and Evelyn, as having been purchased for the pleasure or credit of owning them. Usually they were marvelled at as scientific curiosities or feats of art ('art and mystery' in those days meant what we now call 'craft and trade'). For example, Evelyn referred in 1655 to a 'very extraordinary piece (highly adorn'd)' which was valued at £200 and was in the hands of the Usurper (Cromwell). Its 'balance was onely a chrystall ball'. At all times there have been people with an acquisitive sense about clocks. This was hardly collecting, however, which is deliberately searching for and acquiring particular types of clock.

The truest form of collecting is perhaps to own clocks in order to expand one's knowledge about them, their makers and periods. On rare occasions, a specialist collector will come to know a maker's mind almost as well as his own. Today there are three or four restorers who are able to think like particular 17th- or 18th-century makers and, shown a few holes on the back plate of a complicated clock, will be able to design and make the missing parts, even if no prototypes exist, just as the original clockmaker would have made them. Very few collectors indeed reach this pinnacle of learning, but it exists as an ideal to be striven for.

Anyone who collects almost anything knows that the first questions he will be asked by others will be, 'How old is it?' and 'What's it worth?' There is always the feeling of a skipped heartbeat when one discovers that a find is older and worth more than was suspected when it was purchased, and a sense of achievement when one has successfully negotiated a difficult transaction for a clock. To many the dealing is 'part of the game'. That is why members of collectors' associations deal among themselves and sometimes come into conflict with the professional dealers.

At the same time, making a good bargain is not an end in itself. A collector may pay such a high price that he could only sell at a heavy loss, yet be overjoyed by his purchase, because possessing that particular clock was his only objective.

Clocks attract collectors for exceptionally varied reasons. They are admired as articles of furniture, as decorative metalwork, as antique mechanisms, as modern

ones, for their mechanical ingenuity, for their elegance of design, in a history of science context, as a challenge to keep them going, in a mystical way because they express the concept of time, for their appreciating monetary value, for the apparent companionship they provide, and for many other reasons. There are people who collect clocks of any kind and in any condition just because they are clocks. It is perhaps significant that, when in 1973 the BBC originated a TV series called 'The Fanatics', for their first subject they chose a man whose life was centred on clocks.

Collecting by the layman probably began in the 19th century when the standard of living rose rapidly in England as a result of the Industrial Revolution. So much has been written about certain socially bad aspects of the Industrial Revolution that its incredible achievements have been forgotten by the average man. It made Britain the powerhouse of the world and the pivotal centre of social and economic change affecting every other country. The change from domestic industry to the factory system obviously affected the making of

5 The rolling ball clock was invented by Congreve in 1880, but this version was made by E. Dent & Co., London. It was sold in 1968 for £2,625, more than six times what similar models were being sold for.

A steel ball runs down a zigzag track in a sloping platform in 30 seconds. When it reaches the end, the platform tilts, the hands are advanced and the ball returns.

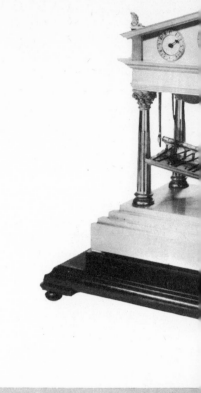

clocks themselves. It stimulated demand for them and, as a reaction, created the desire to collect handmade clocks produced before the machine tool caused so much change in design and 'loss of quality'.

The situation is similar today, except that other countries are leading the Second Industrial Revolution. We are in an even greater period of change, and now familiar machine-made articles, including clocks, will in the years to come be replaced by solid state devices—tiny blocks of plastics with complicated patterns of metal film. Collectors will be seeking today's 'shoddy manufactures' as articles that were 'beautifully designed and assembled, with each part separately made by machine'.

It is in industrial change that the clue to collecting lies. In the earliest period, coinciding with the Renaissance in Europe, every clock was made by an individual or, more often, by several individual craftsmen, each with special skills. Such clocks, dated from the 15th to the mid 17th century, are harder and harder to come by. More and more are being isolated from private collectors, except rich ones, through being acquired by museums.

Overlapping the earliest period was the next, of batch production, in which clocks were still made largely by hand, but in batches of interchangeable parts. It reached its peak in the 18th century and was responsible for the finest work of the English clockmakers. It was also the time when the wooden case rose rapidly to favour and the clock became regarded as a fine piece of furniture rather than a mechanical novelty. This commercial change affected the attitude of the collector in later years when clocks were bought solely for their cases.

The Industrial Revolution in Britain reacted adversely on the clockmaking trade. English clocks were exported in large numbers to, and admired for their excellence in, all parts of the world. (The English lever watch was regarded at the time with the same reverence as the Rolls-Royce in the 20th century.) But the industry was handcraft based, and the workers saw mechanisation as a threat to their jobs; so, strongly affected by Luddite attitudes, they wrecked a factory built to make timepieces by machine. The Industrial Revolution created many new industries and eliminated or severely curtailed those that could not adapt. The French became the dominant clockmaking country because makers concentrated on ornamental metal cases using standard sizes of movements (clock mechanisms) when the Industrial Revolution overtook them after the 1830s. The clock became primarily an ornament for the overfurnished houses of the time.

Subsequently the Americans went through the throes of industrial change in the 1860s. Since they lagged behind European countries in clockmaking and depended heavily on imports of parts and raw materials, they were not so tied to tradition as the Europeans. They

revolutionised the manufacture of timepieces by methods that had to be adopted by other clockmaking communities if they wanted to survive.

At each stage, dyed-in-the-wool collectors were saying that clocks made by the new methods were shoddy and not worth looking at. If there were collectors in 1658 and the following years, the comment was undoubtedly made about the light Dutch wall clocks in wooden cases (they were the first to be controlled by pendulum, the biggest mechanical change for four centuries) when they challenged the heavy ornamental metal German and French clocks of the period. It was no doubt said by owners of London-made clocks about the 'grandfather' clocks with factory-made movements in carpenters' cases, supplied by local 'makers', in the later 18th century. It was certainly said of French Industrial Revolution clocks in metal cases by owners of bracket clocks in wooden cases, and by owners of French clocks when German reproduction clocks imitating French and Austrian clocks came on to the market, and of the floods of cheap American shelf clocks, sold for a few shillings each, which drove the German clocks from the market. Today there are thousands of clocks used for commercial purposes—railway clocks, office clocks and advertising clocks, as well as others for exotic purposes such as time switches and time recorders—that are very often products of fine clockmakers, but are regarded as rubbish by the bulk of people who collect because they are not domestic, not furniture, not very beautiful, not likely to increase soon in price, or because of some other fixed idea. In a decade or two, all will probably have been replaced by mechanical movements made in plastics materials, or by electronic devices: they are no different from the now-valuable 'rubbish' of the past.

It should be pointed out that these words are written about clocks and clock mechanisms that are usually ignored as collectors' items at the time of their manufacture, not about clocks with obvious built-in magnificence in the way of design, ingenuity, sheer skill of making, richness of decoration or material, and so on. Such clocks were never despised and have been admired throughout their existence—and beyond it, if they were, alas, destroyed. They are a warning not to ignore a clock because it is too new or made by methods that are considered too modern. Within the last decade, a London clock- and watchmaking genius constructed some clocks in the manner of one of the greatest makers of all time, A.-L. Breguet (1747–1823). They were considered so perfect by the still existing firm of Breguet, Paris, that they were numbered in the Breguet series. They are new, but stand shoulder to shoulder with the greatest works of the past.

Reproduction clocks have been made for centuries. 4,5,7 Many could not truly be called reproductions: they merely followed a style of fashion to help sell them. Some

7 Reproduction of an English skeleton clock of the late 19th century made commercially today by a Spanish firm, Marton & Gain S.A., of Madrid. It is difficult to distinguish from an original.

8 The marine chronometer is not a reproduction, but a working clock still made today with the skill and precision of a century ago. The only makers left are Thomas Mercer of St Albans, England, who

made this one, Ulysse Nardin of Switzerland, and a state factory in Russia.

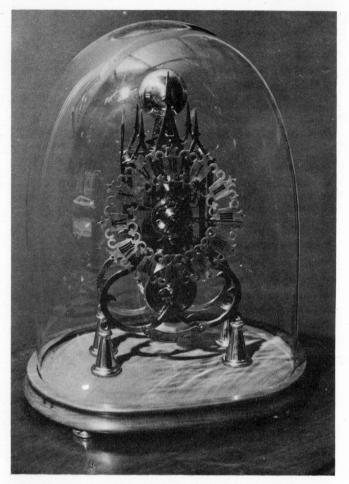

are actual copies. The greatest reproduction period of all time was perhaps that called the 'Second Empire' in France, from 1852 to 1870. It followed the magnificent Empire period from 1800 to 1830, which introduced most of the accepted classical architectural forms for metal clock case ornament. The upheaval of the French Industrial Revolution created a longing for things of the past when life seemed more stable (but was certainly not, because of the French Revolutionary Wars). The new technology of electrotyping was employed to produce many duplicates of Empire period clock cases. Most of the French ormolu clocks seen today are made by a cheaper process of casting in zinc spelter. They are still being made in France.

Fine traditional longcase clocks have been made for many years.

6 Reproductions of traditionally made clocks of high quality and high price began to attract collectors seriously from about 1970, following earlier trends in reproductions of guns, early motor cars and, of course, paintings. There are several current series of reproduction English skeleton clocks that are difficult to distinguish from originals. One of the makers is in Spain. Other clocks reproduced include Congreve rolling ball clocks, hanging ball clocks and rack gravity clocks. Some of the repro-

duction clocks are more expensive than antique versions, but there are always buyers for them, it seems. Certainly they are among the finest clocks made for many years, and as genuine antiques become rarer so will the demand for faithful reproductions increase, despite their rising cost. At the same time, the reproductions are certain to retain their values.

There is another category of high quality modern clock, in the finest traditions of the past, but not a reproduction. An example is the chronometer clock for home use made like a marine chronometer. Some of 8 these, and some reproductions, are in limited editions only.

Finally, there is a modern form of clock that is a collector's item, but defies exact classification. Such clocks are called 'horological sculptures' by one of their makers, Martin Burgess, because they are built for special customers and situations, as well as for their aesthetic qualities, like sculpture. His own clocks are elegantly designed large exposed clock mechanisms that incorporate classical horological devices.

A first purchase of a clock may be for any reason, but it will most likely be as an ornament. Subsequent purchases may be at random, but a serious collector usually has some objective. He may collect clocks of a particular nationality or a particular type of clock.

For different people and at different times, either the case or the movement has been of primary interest. The making of each involved different skills, which hints at one way of discovering an original approach to collecting. What other skills are there that could provide the primary interest of a collector and perhaps lead him to becoming a specialist in some aspect of horology? A fairly obvious one is dials, almost invariably made by specialists. Enamelled dials, for example, were used on earlier French clocks, with twelve, or more rarely with thirteen, separate cartouches for the chapters (the hour numerals), with a central one sometimes making the thirteenth. Large enamelled dials are not often seen. Very 13 occasionally one is encountered on a longcase clock, more often on a continental regulator (a high precision clock). To concentrate on decorative enamelled dials could be rewarding, although perhaps expensive.

At the lower priced end of the market, what about studying clocks with wooden or paper dials? Many were made by the first German factories in the Black Forest and by early American factories.

A new look at American shelf clocks could create a fresh interest. Forget for a moment the case and the clock, and consider the reverse-painted glass that is a peculiarity of many earlier American clocks. Some were painted by hand and are works of art in their own right. Others were transfers from prints, laid by one or other of the methods described in a book *Polygraphice* by William Salmon, published in London in 1701. Many

American clock glasses covering the dial and the pendulum have borders of gold leaf in filigree pattern on the back of the glass, decorated with coloured paints. These glass paintings are called 'verres églomisés', after Eglomi, the Parisian picture framer who invented the method in the late 17th century.

Another idea is to concentrate on clocks with wooden movements. Quantities of them were made in the Black Forest, in Germany, and are not difficult to find. Many were also made in America, from about 1790. The wheels themselves make an interesting study. At first, in mid 18th century, they were cut by hand tools, such as chisels. Some clockmakers used a milling cutter similar to that for brass wheels. Then, probably first in America around 1806 by Eli Terry, a sawing technique was introduced and rapidly became general. Wooden clocks were made in England as early as 1713, but not because metal was unobtainable, or for cheapness. They were the work of the carpenters John and James Harrison. (John was the first to design extremely high precision clocks that would work in sailing ships and, as a result, made accurate navigation possible and the Royal Navy supreme.) The wooden wheels had the teeth cut in a series of trianguiar pieces of wood joined together in a circle so that the grain was radial. One of the Harrisons'

longcase clocks can be seen in the Worshipful Company of Clockmakers' collection in the Guildhall, City of London.

Travelling or coaching clocks have been made for centuries and have a special attraction of their own, as exemplified by the French carriage clock, which has rocketed in price in very recent years because it was 'discovered' by the general public rather than collectors as such. In the same area, railway clocks would make an interesting theme, especially if associated with old time-tables giving conversions from local time (when there was no Greenwich Time and every part of the country had its own time) to Railway Time. The Americans made special clocks for fitting to railway engines.

What about security clocks? Probably no one collects them. They would include not only time locks for safes and watchman's clocks, but pigeon clocks that prevent the 'fixing' of pigeon races, even money banks, savings clocks, and cigarette cases with time locks to reduce nicotine consumption!

These suggestions only touch the edge of the huge area of interest that clocks can generate. There are many aspects still to be explored at almost every period of clockmaking, from the early days of the 14th century to the hardly examined early 20th.

Where to find, and find out about, clocks

9 Many water clocks like this can be found with a float in a water chamber that turns the hands as the water leaks out to a tank below. Many have dates on them, from 1660 to 1702. None is genuine and most were made by the Birmingham firm of Pearson, Page & Jewsbury.

Where does one find clocks worth buying to start a collection? There are more antique shops selling them today than at any other time, owing to the increasing interest of the public in clocks, so that there is no lack of opportunity. Unfortunately, few dealers in antiques know anything serious about clocks, and many have little idea of the condition of the pieces they sell – only of the prices they require. There are specialist dealers who are knowledgeable about clocks and take care to ensure that the movements are in as good order as it is possible to make them. It is usually best to buy from these specialists until one is knowledgeable enough to bank on one's own judgement of authenticity, quality and price, unless, of course, the search is for clocks or movements outside the normal specialists' interest or quality and price range. Curiously, prices in furniture-based dealers' shops are often higher than in specialists'; in fact, antique furniture dealers usually make the running at auctions for 'furnishing clocks' during a period of rising prices because they disregard the condition of movements.

Auctions are the place for the knowledgeable collector to buy, either by bidding himself or through an agent. At the more important auctions, it is sometimes more advantageous financially to buy through a dealer because dealers may try to shut out a private bidder by pushing up prices. Both Sotheby's and Christie's have regular sales of furniture and clocks and, from time to time, special sales for important clocks only. Sotheby's Belgravia holds regular sales of later clocks and other articles made between 1830 and 1930, at their London auction rooms, and also list expected bidding ranges before the sale. There are also sales of antiques, including clocks, in London by Jackson, Stops & Staff and other major auctioneers, and overseas by Sotheby Parke Bernet Inc. in New York, Christie's in Geneva, Galerie am Neumarkt in Geneva (which publishes useful catalogues with valuations), and many others. A valuable investment is to subscribe to Christie's and Sotheby's illustrated catalogues of auctions containing clocks. After the auctions, lists of prices realised are provided. An advantage of buying from one of the top auction rooms is that the articles for sale are vetted by experts. Both Christie's and Sotheby's have specialist horological consultants who are practical restorers and makers of clocks as well as being antiquarians.

Another source of supply is the antique fair. These fairs are held regularly in many parts of the country and sometimes turn up an unexpected and exciting find for the collector. At some smaller fairs and certainly at the Grosvenor House Antiques Fair, the biggest on the yearly calendar, exhibits are vetted for authenticity.

Despite the vetting, the eagle-eyed collector can still occasionally find a 'wrong 'un' and also a bargain. At one of the top London auctions in London in 1972, there

were not one but *two* extremely rare 16th-century clocks with what are called cross-beat escapements that slipped through without special notice although they were recognised by a Dutch expert. In the nick of time, the British Museum managed to enter a bid and acquire one, but the other was bought by a private collector.

As well as being protected by initial examination by specialists to avoid errors, the buyer in the United Kingdom also has the shelter of the Trade Descriptions Act. A trader cannot lawfully offer for sale an article described as 18th-century when it was made in the 19th, a practice not uncommon with furniture. If in doubt, the buyer should insist on a written description on the receipt. In 1972 an antique dealer was convicted of describing an old clock as 'in working order' when it was not, according to experts called to give evidence for the Trading Standards Department.

The Trade Descriptions Act also affects descriptions of lots in auction catalogues. The top auction rooms have always been cautious with descriptions and since the Act have been especially careful. This unfortunately tends to make many descriptions vague; in fact, the vaguer the description, the more carefully the item should be scrutinised before bidding. There are certain conventions in auction room descriptions, such as giving an artist's surname only to indicate that a picture was painted *not* by him, but by one of his followers or in his style; fortunately the clock buyer does not normally have to contend with such saleroom shorthand, but might have to if the clock is in a valuable ceramic case, because the same conventions are followed in ceramics.

Prices of better antique clocks in auctions rose steeply during 1971 and 1972, bringing them more into line with paintings and ceramics. There was a similar adjustment upwards in the 1950s, when European buyers discovered the wealth of 'low-priced' antique clocks in Britain. After that time top prices occasionally exceeded £10,000. After the last upwards surge, top prices sometimes exceeded £15,000. These high peaks tended to suck up prices right through the antique range, to the currently low-priced end of the furnishing market in French black marble mantel clocks and machine-made Regency pattern mantel clocks of the early part of the 20th Century.

It pays to buy quality if appreciation in value is an important consideration. An 18th-century English clock in good condition, with nothing missing from the movement and with the name of a recorded maker on the dial, may be expensive but will also be certain to appreciate at a higher rate than a similar clock which is deficient in one way or another.

The name on the dial has always been important to clock dealers and to most collectors, largely because it signifies the approximate date of the clock. Most clock-making countries, particularly Germany, France and England, had craft guilds that controlled the apprenticeship and training of would-be clockmakers. In England, early clockmakers generally belonged to the guild of blacksmiths, and in other countries to that of the blacksmiths or locksmiths, until their own guilds were formed. In England, this was on 22nd August 1631, when the Company of Clockmakers was incorporated by Royal Charter granted by King Charles I. The Company's records fortunately escaped the Great Fire of London in 1666 and are now preserved entirely intact in the Guildhall Library, London. From them, the Company publishes in book form a Register of Apprentices from 1631 to 1931, which is valuable for dating signed English clocks.

Books are invaluable to the collector, and the object of the book you are now reading is to help people with an interest in collecting clocks. It is obviously too short to do more than this, to give some guidance in the direction in which the reader's interests may lie, some hints on seeking and looking after clocks, and a general history of the mechanical clock. A history of timekeeping on a broader historical plan is provided by the author's *Clocks and Watches*, also published by Hamlyn.

Not much general help will be found in early books on clocks, which were almost invariably concerned with technical matters; a few were philosophical, and a very few gave examples of case designs. The first book mainly concerned with collecting was probably *Former Clock and Watchmakers and Their Work*, by F. J. Britten. The first edition appeared in 1894. Britten was the secretary of the British Horological Institute, which had been formed in Clerkenwell in 1858. The book attracted sufficient interest for Britten to enlarge and revise it to become his *Old Clocks and Watches and Their Makers*, first published in 1898. This is the book that, in any of its editions up to the sixth, is referred to by collectors and the trade as 'Britten'. The seventh edition of 1956 was completely revised and is a valuable, although different, kind of book. Much of Britten's information came from early editions of the Institute's official journal, *The Horological Journal*, and can be recognised as 'scissor-and-paste work', but that did not detract from his book's value. Early editions are now collector's pieces in themselves.

The value of old copies of Britten is in the large number of illustrations and descriptions of actual clocks. A disadvantage is that some of the facts and suppositions of the time when it was written are now known to be untrue. For example, a water clock dated 1682 is described as 'original and a fine example of the period'. In fact it is a fake, and many such clocks are known to exist. Moreover, the clock was a pure invention of early in this century and has no ancestor.

Britten's book was followed in 1913 by another that had a strong influence on clock collecting and clock collectors for several decades. It was entitled *English*

Domestic Clocks and was written by Herbert Cescinsky, a specialist in antique furniture, and Malcolm R. Webster, a specialist clock dealer. It was reprinted by Spring Books in 1969. Cescinsky subsequently wrote another book, *The Old English Master Clockmakers and their Clocks,* which reinforced the interest he created in the case rather than the clock. He admired a clock solely because of its case and presumably would have admired a picture solely because of its frame. This attitude persisted among collectors and buyers to such an extent that auction prices of clocks became depressed, although no one realised it, until the invasion of continental buyers in the 1950s. There was a time when a longcase clock, bought as a piece of furniture by a collector, cost less than, say, a chair, because its horological value—the fact that it was a magnificent example of an 18th-century *clock*—was to a large extent ignored.

Another valuable, indeed essential, book for clock collectors is not a book in the ordinary sense, but a list of makers. It is known in the trade as 'the Book' or as 'Baillie'. G. H. Baillie was an engineer and physicist who became absorbed by the history of clock- and watch-making and spent a great deal of his time and a considerable sum of money researching collections and early horological literature in order to compile an authentic list of 36,000 clock and watchmakers from the earliest days until 1825, with their dates, places of work, and other basic information. It is called *Watchmakers and Clockmakers of the World* (NAG Press) and can be consulted in most public libraries. Baillie also compiled a bibliography of abstracts and summaries of horological references in books and pamphlets, which is very valuable for the research worker.

There are many names not in 'Baillie', and this at times upsets dealers and owners. The reason may have been, and in some cases is known to have been, because Baillie did not come across the maker. Most omitted names were excluded deliberately, however. It was common in the later 18th and 19th century for the name of the retailer (who still called himself a 'clockmaker') to be engraved or painted on the dial and often engraved on the brass back plate of the movement. The practice was so common that Baillie deliberately suppressed many names he found to be those of retailers. Clockmaking factories in London and Birmingham during the period engraved or painted on a 'maker's' name to order as normal practice. Records of Thwaites & Reed of Clerkenwell in possession of the Worshipful Company of Clockmakers even list many famous genuine makers to whom they supplied clock movements in this way. The famous makers supplied factory-made clocks as their 'cheap lines' in the 18th century.

For collectors interested in French clocks, a valuable volume is *La Pendule Française,* by Tardy, published in Paris. It comprises a large number of illustrations gleaned from every possible source and reprinted from all kinds of material. Some are badly reproduced, but at least a huge variety of clocks is shown in periods with brief captions in French.

The clock collector must obviously have some general reference works, and he could hardly do better than to follow the recommendations in the British Museum publication *Clocks in the British Museum* by Hugh Tait, which is itself an essential book, being a very valuable thesis on the development of the mechanical clock. Baillie and Britten are listed plus the 'new Britten', with the same title, by G. H. Baillie, C. Clutton and C. A. Ilbert. Another book by F. J. Britten, *Watch and Clockmaker's Handbook,* follows because of the useful technical information it contains. Cescinsky and Webster's book is listed, as are two catalogues, that of the Science Museum, London, by Dr F. A. B. Ward, called *Time Measurement,* and the catalogue of 'The British Clockmaker's Heritage' exhibition, held at the Science Museum in 1952. A book that should be added to the list is *Investing in Clocks and Watches* by P. G. Cumhail, a nom-de-plume of the late Philip Coole of the British Museum.

Other books suggested are two by the present author, *The Longcase Clock,* and *Clocks and Watches, 1400–1900,* plus *The Grandfather Clock* by E. L. Edwardes, *The Knibb Family, Clockmakers* by R. A. Lee, *Old Clocks,* 3rd edition, by H. A. Lloyd, and *Thomas Tompion, His Life and Work* by R. W. Symonds.

Reading about clocks is only a start. Next they must be seen, then handled and finally, for many enthusiasts, taken apart and put together again. Many of today's enthusiasts owe their initial experience to a remarkable man named Courtenay A. Ilbert, who died in 1956. For one reason or another they had found their way to Ilbert's crumbling old mansion in Chelsea, where every room was occupied by multitudes of clocks that are now national treasures in the British Museum. The collection was virtually a complete history of clockmaking from the year 1500 to the start of mass production. Courtenay Ilbert was intensely shy and had little ability in explanation, yet his knowledge was immense and he rarely had to refer to his remarkable library that backed up the clocks. The library of horological books, the world's finest, he bequeathed to the British Horological Institute.

There were always visitors in Ilbert's house, it seemed, taking a clock to pieces, making notes, talking, arguing. He was so generous of knowledge and in lending his most valuable clocks that it seemed to be a self-imposed duty to compensate for his fortune in life. Some priceless specimens were damaged as a result of his generosity notably some treasures with automata that were lent for exhibition on the continent and were returned badly damaged and without thanks.

Today the lucky collector can see, and even examine, clocks in the world-famous Ilbert Collection by going to the British Museum. When the Museum acquired the collection of clocks (and later the watches)—by means of a large financial gift from Mr Gilbert Edgar, later the Master of the Worshipful Company of Clockmakers, by public subscription, and through Museum funds—a Students' Room for Horological and Scientific Instruments was set up at the Museum to provide ideal facilities for apprentices, collectors and students to study the material. The Ilbert Room is unique.

The collector can, too, study the Ilbert Library, which was in London for a number of years, but is now housed at the headquarters of the British Horological Institute at Upton Park, Newark, Nottinghamshire.

To understand books or clocks themselves with any depth of understanding, one has to learn some of the language of horology. Clockmaking is a mechanical aspect of horology (the art and science of timekeeping) and is the oldest practice of precision engineering, except perhaps in 'engineering' itself, which consisted of inventing engines of war. Some practitioners, notably Leonardo da Vinci in the 15th century, concerned themselves deeply with both.

Clockmaking is a single-minded activity. Over five centuries of intense effort in imagination and skill of hand have been spent with the sole objective of making a hand go round a dial at the same rate as the Sun 'goes round' the Earth. When, in the 17th century, the clock triumphed over the Sun in accuracy, the clockmakers took on the stars and in the 20th century beat them for accuracy too. For this dedication, they surely have a right to their own language. It has hardly changed throughout the centuries in any tongue and is as stubbornly precise today.

Already in these first few words a specialised term—rate—has been employed. To a clockmaker, the 'rate' is the regularity of the going of the clock, not whether or not it shows the right time. If a clock loses, say, a minute a day, no more, no less, day after day without variation, it has a perfect rate. A clock that loses a minute one day, gains half a minute the next, and in fact varies in its timekeeping, has a bad rate. It may still show the correct time of day months later, while the clock with the good rate will be an hour or more slow, but at any time it is possible to obtain an accurate time of day from the clock with the good rate.

When the first mechanical clocks were invented, in medieval times, the regularity of work and prayers was controlled by bell-ringing. (The word 'clock' comes from the French 'cloche' (bell) because the early clocks struck a single note at each hour; and, since this was their sole purpose, many even had no dial.) Even outside the monasteries, villagers were notified of the evening curfew (putting out of fires) by the ringing of a bell. The sexton or watchman was warned of the time to ring the

bell by the earliest form of mechanical clock, the alarm. As happens today in other occupations, over the years sextons and watchmen became lazy or inefficient and were replaced by machines. In this case, they were superseded by large models of men who struck the large bells formerly tolled by real men. In 1410, it was reported not only that the 'striker of the hours by night and day' in the French town of Montpellier struck them incorrectly but that his wages were too high; so the town council replaced him by an automatic wooden man called 'Jacomart' they bought from Dijon, who struck the hours correctly. The name 'jack' is commonly used today by clockmakers for an automaton imitating a human being. There is a medieval one still working at Wells cathedral, made in 1392 and called 'Jack Blandifer'. This may seem remote from practical clock collecting, but domestic clocks with automata are still to be found.

The clock movement (mechanism) was built in a frame, comprising four posts at the corners linked by bars to hold the clockwork itself. Then plates were introduced top and bottom. Soon after 1650, a clockmaker turned the plates through 90°, so that they were at back and front; posts uniting them became known as pillars.

Mounted between the plates of such a plated clock

12 The botcher has been at work on this clock plate. The pivot holes were worn and, instead of drilling them out to a larger size and pressing in bushes with the correct holes, the botcher has punched around the worn holes to squeeze them smaller. The practice takes much value from a movement.

13 Unusual English bracket clock with an enamel dial signed 'Henry Jenkins, Cheapside No. 1352'. The movement is signed 'Thos Haley, London', who arrived from Norwich in 1761. According to 'Baillie', Jenkins worked in London from about 1730 to 1788.

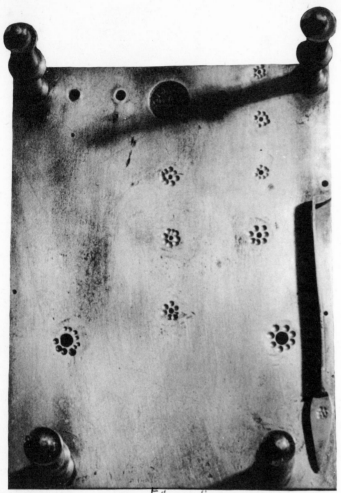

movement are the driving wheels (the word 'cog' makes a clockmaker shudder). The teeth of the brass wheels engage with the "leaves" (teeth) of small steel wheels called pinions (generally a larger 'wheel' drives a smaller 'pinion'). Wheels and pinions are fixed not to shafts but to arbors. All the shafts (except two) are known as arbors.

One might expect engineers to understand clocks more readily than laymen, despite the difference in terms, but this is not so. Engineers have the preconceived idea that a machine is an apparatus to convert one form of energy into another to do useful work. Brought up, maybe, on Samuel Smiles' *Lives of the Engineers* and *Self-help,* they do not readily accept the idea of a machine that wastes its time; but that is exactly what a clock does. All the energy stored in a clock by a weight or a coiled spring is consumed by friction, by swinging a balance wheel or bar or a pendulum to and fro and absorbing the momentum of other moving parts, and by the noise of ticking. If a clock is efficient, it has little surplus power and therefore will be quiet and will be stopped by lack of oil on pivots (the bearings at the ends of arbors that run in holes in the plates) or worn holes. It may also be stopped by oil in the wrong places. It has been known for a spider's web to stop a big tower or turret clock.

All mechanical clocks work in little jumps, and the tick and tock are sounds caused by the escapement, which intercepts a wheel, bringing the clock movement to a halt after it has been released, usually every second in a longcase clock, or at shorter intervals in smaller and longer intervals in large turret clocks. If a clock is designed to use a lot of power, all of this will have to be dispersed in absorbed momentum, friction and noise, so the parts will have to be bigger and stronger to resist the extra loading and extra wear. The finest clocks therefore consume little power and have carefully designed, strong but light, moving parts made to fine tolerances, that will often last for centuries.

The direct relevance of this to collecting clocks is that a finely made clock is usually an efficient one. In a well-made weight-driven clock, a heavier weight was employed by some clockmakers to drive a striking or chiming train than a 'going' train (which drives the hands), so weights should be labelled if removed, or weighed if there is any doubt about which is which. Not infrequently an unfeeling repairer will change a weight for a heavier one instead of rebushing worn holes or 12 carrying out other work on the clock to reduce friction. A high quality clock made to run for a month will often have a lighter weight than a 30-hour longcase clock.

A 'train' means a group of engaging wheels and pinions. The going train drives not only the hands but also pendulum or other oscillator. A separate striking train drives the hammer that strikes the hour bell and is released at the correct times by the going train. A chiming train is likewise separate and released when required. In a striking clock, the going train (and winding square which accepts the key) is normally on the right and the striking train (and its winding square) on the left. A chiming train, if incorporated, is normally planted in the middle of a posted frame clock, but on the extreme right if the clock is key-wound.

The rate of going of a clock depends upon its time controller—most frequently a pendulum in an antique clock. The pendulum is given regular impulses in one or both directions, to keep it swinging, by means of an escapement operating on the last wheel in the going train, known as the escape wheel. The pendulum's main function is to release the clock train at measured intervals to allow the hands to jump forwards. Every hand moves in jumps that are easily seen with a seconds hand, but not so readily with the minute hand and not at all with the hour hand. Each jump means that the pendulum has released the escapement and the escape wheel has jumped the hands forward and impulsed the pendulum. Also, the driving weight has dropped very slightly and has been stopped with a jerk, or the mainspring has uncoiled a little.

Other terms will be explained as they are introduced.

The early period

Before the pendulum

14 The large iron clock from Cassiobury Park (Herts.). It has a cockleshell mark on the central crossbar. There are other clocks with such a mark in Clandon Park; St Peter's church, Buntingford (Herts.); over the stables at Quickswood farm (Herts.) and elsewhere. They have been dated as 16th-century, but a detailed description of how to make them appeared in Brussels in about 1400.

The earliest clocks were large iron constructions mounted inside monasteries, churches, church towers, curfew towers and stately homes. A few famous ones which are thought to be the earliest, fine examples of their time, or earliest known with a technical improvement, are now in museums. Most of those in England belong to the ecclesiastical authorities. They are easily recognisable from illustrations, but to appreciate their size it is best to make a point of seeing a medieval clock, such as the Cassiobury Park clock in the British Museum, probably made in the 14th century; the clock at Salisbury cathedral, the earliest still going, almost certainly made in 1386; the still-working Exeter cathedral clock that operates an astronomical dial; or that at Wimbourne minster, Dorset, also with an operational astronomical dial; the clock jacks and astronomical dial at Wells cathedral, Somerset, and its movement in the Science Museum, London; or the clock in Rye church, Sussex, which recent research dates back to the 14th century. There are many others scattered round southern England.

In church towers there are still very many ancient clocks. Unfortunately members of the clergy are often ignorant or unappreciative of the horological treasures in their care. In 1972, the committee of the Council for the Care of Places of Worship concerned with clocks heard of a medieval clock that had been relegated to a scrap heap as a 'pile of old iron' by the local parson. Fortunately it was rescued just before the scrap merchant arrived. Others disappeared before their fate was known. Many have had original parts removed and scrapped in order to fit electric motors to drive the hands, a practice strictly forbidden without the express permission of higher Church authority. It would be a service to the history of horology and the preservation of the country's treasures if those interested in and knowledgeable about clocks made a point of seeing as many old church clocks as possible and interesting the local incumbents in their preservation, if they are not already aware of the age and value of the clocks.

It might be thought that the earliest clocks were out of the grasp of today's collector, but that is not so. Early wrought iron clocks that have come on the market because a big house has been demolished, or an old clock replaced by a new one, have been neglected because of their size and because they could not be regarded as furniture. Iron mechanisms are now considered to be decorative.

At a recent Chelsea Antiques Fair a medieval iron vertical clock made before 1550 was offered at a price many an ordinary collector could afford. Unfortunately it was sold to someone who wanted it for decorating a room before at least one serious collector could offer for it. In the antique shops of Camden Passage in north London while this book was being written, there were four old turret clocks for sale.

Briefly, the chronology of turret clocks follows this sequence in relation to construction (the dates are of course only approximate):

14th–17th centuries 'Birdcage' construction. Made of 14 wrought iron strips held together by wedges, with large wrought iron wheels and wooden barrels around which ropes were wound to drive the clock and striking mechanism.

The earlier the clock, the more robust the frame. Very early frames had the corner posts set at 45° and were shaped like church buttresses at the bottom and decorated by knobs or in some other way at the top. The later the clock, the less the decoration. Before about 1658, all such clocks were controlled by a slowly oscillating horizontal bar with a weight at each end (the foliot), but almost all were converted to pendulum at some time in their history.

1400–1550 Vertical frame clocks. These were a peculiarly English form of turret clock, with the wrought iron wheels in a vertical line up a single post. They were made in the West Country with iron frames and in the Midlands with wooden frames. The construction is similar to the earliest German small iron wall clocks of the earlier 15th century.

18th–19th centuries 'Bedpost' construction. The style, in cast iron, of the corner posts is immediately reminiscent of a Victorian bedstead. The wheels are usually of brass or bronze. When large, bedpost clocks are too big and heavy for most people to consider buying, but small ones about 20 inches wide exist. Many clocks from

15 Iron German or possibly Dutch clock
with a painted dial and side door decorated
inside as well as outside. The main dial is a
'double-twelve'—a 24-hour dial marked I
to XII twice. Inner dials indicate signs of
the zodiac and phases of the Moon.

16 A very early German iron monastic
alarm that hangs on the wall. The frame
comprises two vertical bars held by
horizontal ones top and bottom fixed by
tapered pins. The driving weight, not
shown, operates a foliot escapement, visible

under the bell, with an adjustable weight
at each end. The single hand indicates
hours, and dots show half hours. The tail of
the hand indicates the alarm setting on the
rotatable central disc.

the later 18th century have the date of manufacture cast into the frame.

19th–20th centuries Flatbed frame. The wheels, of cast iron or brass or bronze, are set in a line in bearings along a horizontal frame. The idea was French and first adopted in Britain for the 'Big Ben' clock in 1858. It would be difficult to collect something the size of Big Ben's movement, the length of a small railway engine! Small neat flatbed movements that are less than two feet long can

be sought and bought and are much easier to deal with.

Large iron-framed clocks for sounding the times of church services, to warn villagers of curfew, of fire outbreaks and, round the coasts, of invasion, were common on the continent where they originated, but far more have been preserved in England than elsewhere. On the continent, the iron-framed clock was scaled down for use by important public officials and richer families, to become the first domestic clocks. The earliest German 17

17 A Gothic iron clock, the domestic clock of the 16th century. The dial is painted and the corner posts are set at an angle of 45° like those of the even earlier big iron public clocks. The lower hand shows quarter hours. Control is by a foliot, seen at the top, with a weight at each end to alter the rate.

small iron clocks were not of true frame construction, but were made from two or three vertical bars united by a bar at the top and another at the bottom. A cross-piece at the bottom with two 'spars' stopped the clock from rocking when hung on the wall. A similar construction, but with a base, was used in Italy. In the 15th century, the iron chamber clock had a regular four-posted frame and was made in France and Germany. The hour was shown by a single hand, often on a painted iron front panel, the hour was sounded on a bell, often there was an alarm, the controller was an oscillating foliot bar with an adjustable weight at each end to alter timekeeping, and the drive was by a weight or weights.

Gothic clocks, as they were called, were made from iron throughout the 16th century and into the 17th. They are now rare and one appears only very occasionally at an auction.

The first English domestic clock was of similar general construction in that it had four corner posts like the earliest iron clocks, with the wheels and their arbors set between vertical straps, but the clock was much smaller, the mechanism was enclosed, and the outer parts were made of brass, then known as 'latten'. The brass or latten clock has become corrupted into the 'lantern' clock. Lantern clocks perhaps first appeared in about 1600 and were fully developed by about 1630. Usually the feet and finials (the decorations on the top corners) screwed into the pillars and thereby held top and bottom plates in place. Less commonly feet and finials were integral with the posts; the plates were slotted in and held by tapered pins. Lantern clocks were being made in much the same outward form in the beginning of the 20th century. In fact, versions of them can be seen in modern catalogues and are similar superficially, although the movement is very different.

All early lantern clocks were driven by weights. All had the bell on the top. Although the clock spring was introduced about a century before the lantern clock era, only modern English lantern clocks are driven by spring. The true lantern clock was a practical timekeeper for general use that could be made to a reasonable price for the time.

All lantern clocks made before about 1660 had an oscillating wheel or a foliot balance at the top under the bell, to regulate the timekeeping.

The balance (the word covers both wheel and foliot types) releases the clock movement at every swing and is itself impulsed (given a small push) at every swing to keep it in motion. The link between the balance and the driving wheels of the clock is the device already referred to, the escapement. In the lantern clock, in every earlier type of mechanical clock and in very many later ones, the escapement comprises a crown wheel driven by the clock and a verge connected to the balance. The verge is the staff (shaft) of the balance and has two small 'flags',

16

20

24

18 Lantern clock movements were made from 1660 to almost 1800, the later ones having square or break-arch dials and used on a bracket, under a hood, on a wall or in a long case. This one was made in about 1760 by Isaac Rogers of London for the Turkish market. It has a verge with short pendulum.

19 The pillar movement of a south German tabernacle clock similar to that in plate 25. This one is driven by a spring and fusee and is controlled by a one-arm balance wheel.

called pallets, projecting from it. It is mounted across the crown wheel (so called because of its saw teeth liken it to a traditional king's crown) so that the pallets intercept a tooth at every swing of the balance. In an early lantern clock, the crown wheel is mounted so that it is in the same vertical plane as the other wheels of the clock.

The slowly oscillating foliot type of balance, with an adjustable weight at each end to alter its rate, working with a crown wheel and verge escapement, can be seen in action at the British Museum, which has a gallery showing the development of clock movements, most of which are kept going. The foliot was followed by the balance wheel with a single spoke.

When the idea of employing a short pendulum instead of a balance arrived in England from Holland in 1658, it was so successful that lantern clocks were made with short pendulums.

A long pendulum looks incongruous hanging behind a small brass lantern clock on a wall shelf or hung on the wall, but it is absolutely 'right' historically because thousands of lantern clocks were converted to anchor escapement and long pendulum operation after 1670 and thousands of others were made that way. The finials dissapeared, and the movement was mounted in a (usually ungainly) wooden long case. Occasionally one is seen mounted in the Japanese manner on a pyramid-shaped stand, usually made of oak, that hid the weights and long pendulum.

The earlier lantern clock for hanging on a wall had at the back of the frame a half-hoop-shaped piece at the top for fitting over a hook, and two pointed spurs (like the first German iron domestic clocks) for holding the clock away from the wall. They prevented it from moving, because they dug into the wall, while being wound by pulling on the ropes that held the weights.

A lantern clock had one weight for the timekeeping or going train, another for striking and sometimes a third smaller one for an alarm. A weight was held by a cord round a pulley with a V-groove. Friction in the pulley groove, very often assisted by a series of sharp spikes, and a smaller weight on the other end kept it from slipping. This system replaced the earlier one on Gothic clocks, in about 1500. The earlier method was to have two cords wound round halves of a barrel in opposite directions. One held the driving weight and wound up the other which was held by a small weight. Pulling the small-weighted line wound up the other. Turret clocks have barrels, but with a single weight line, to this day.

On the continent, the early iron Gothic clocks continued to be the main weight-driven timekeeper for domestic use, but iron clocks more like the English lantern clock were also made. However, a rival was appearing in greater and greater numbers—the portable

25

20 Unsigned English brass lantern clock of about 1660 in original condition, with hanging eye and spurs at the back and one-arm balance wheel. The dolphin fret was a popular device.

21 The back of the lantern clock showing the balance wheel under the bell. Most of these clocks were converted to pendulum operation, a few to verge and short pendulum after about 1660, but most to

anchor escapement and long pendulum after 1675.

clock driven by a coiled spring instead of a weight. The mainspring was in regular use in 1550, having been invented about 70 years earlier, probably in Burgundy. The first spring-driven clocks were built like weight clocks in a vertical 'four-poster' frame, but plates were added to top and bottom to which side, front and back plates could be fastened to form a case. The springs were in the base, and drove the clock through 'fusees' (explained later, on page 29). The earliest known is dated about 1480 and is now in the British Museum. It was subsequently converted to weight drive, but a scale model shows how it once worked.

Spring-driven, posted-frame table clocks became relatively common in the late 16th and early 17th centuries. One version, made in southern Germany, was monumental in form and about three feet high to its central spike, and is today called a 'tabernacle clock'. The copper and bronze gilt cases are elaborately engraved and chased, and the bell on top is surmounted by a tower carried on pillars, or there is a series of canopies. More than one dial is quite usual, and very occasionally tiny figures (jacks) or other automata strike the bell or bells.

Tabernacle clocks are not likely to be encountered in an antique shop, but they do appear at better-known auctions from time to time. Most of those outside museums are electrotype copies, which were made in some numbers in the 19th century.

Some early spring clocks were made with elaborate astronomical mechanisms and a number of dials indicating calendar information, the positions of the Sun and the Moon in the Zodiac, positions of certain stars, as well as the phase, aspect and age of the Moon. A few even provided striking on the 6- or the 24-hour system, and an indication of time according to all three systems in use in Europe around 1650. It would seem impossible to find such an exciting clock today, but a few years ago one was recognised for what it was in a stately home, where it had been 'lost' for years among the furniture.

Parallel with the making of four-poster spring-driven clocks came a development that was more profound than was realised. It was the horizontal spring-driven table clock. The arbors bearing the wheels of the clock were turned through a right angle and made to run in bearings in the top and bottom plates, instead of in the supports that held the top and bottom plates together, so that the dial was on top.

The first of these plate frame clocks were made about 1460 and were round. A wheel driving through a right angle, called a 'contrate wheel', was introduced so as to plant the balance parallel to the plates. No striking was incorporated, but a separate alarm was provided if required. It stood on three legs over the horizontal dial and was released by a trigger on the timepiece. These drum-shaped clocks were French, Flemish and German.

Later some makers introduced square and hexagonal shapes. Most of those still existing are German, with 24-hour dials. French ones have 12-hour dials. Recently some hexagonal table clocks have come up for auction.

The design was especially significant because, made smaller and hung on a chain, it became the first personal timekeeper, the watch.

Makers of table clocks, from about 1550, in Augsburg particularly, combined them with animated figures. They also varied the dial from a small indicator to a figure pointing at a moving dial. Their production of novelty clocks seems astonishing to us now, but it was the time of the Renaissance, with the blossoming of art in Europe.

French and Flemish makers developed a small spring-driven table clock with horizontal plates—sometimes three of them to make a two-tiered clock—but with a vertical dial. The clock is usually square or hexagonal with a bell on top and stands only a few inches high.

22 A drum-shaped table clock of about 1696. The case was cut from a solid piece of rock crystal. The alarm mechanism is separate and stands on three feet on top of the horizontal dial. It is separately spring-driven and triggered by the hour hand of the drum clock.

23 Movement of a clock made by Jacob the Zech (it means 'the younger'), which is believed to be the earliest in existence with a fusee drive. The tapered fusee barrel can be seen at top left. Diagonally across the centre of the movement is a foliot with a weight at each end that can be screwed in or out. The clock is dated about 1525.

Some continental makers who had emigrated to England also made them in London.

Table clocks, the ones that still exist outside museums, are usually offered for sale by auction and are almost invariably expensive. Some superb examples exist in private collections, as well as in museums. Among the 29 most fascinating are the so-called Orpheus clocks, the cases of which were made from a band which was cast in bronze with decoration showing Orpheus and Euridice at the entrance to Hades. Nine such clocks are known, seven round and two square. Eight are in private collections and museums. What so interests the specialist is that although the clock movements were produced by different clockmakers in different places, the decorative strip came out of the same workshop (although other parts of the cases did not), so there must have been a workshop, probably in Augsburg or Nuremberg in south Germany, supplying the clock trade with decorative strip as early as the 16th century, which shows how industrialised the trade had already become.

The ninth Orpheus clock is known to exist because it was photographed. After about 1900, however, it appears to have disappeared. It could have been destroyed, but probably it is in a loft or cellar somewhere waiting for someone to discover it. It is square and has a lunar dial.

Domestic clocks before the pendulum fall into these general periods:

From about 1300 Clocks and alarms built on vertical frames with revolving dials or single hands. Large painted iron clocks without cases, for domestic use. All weight-driven.

From about 1450 Small and large spring-driven vertical table clocks in metal cases. Spring-driven horizontal table clocks (i.e. with dial on top).

1500–1600 Many varieties of spring and weight clocks. 30 From mid century, the simpler form of domestic clock was relatively commonplace, and makers turned their efforts to more novelty and more decoration, introducing music-playing, astrolabic (star-measuring) and other 24 dials, moving figures and figures with moving eyes. Most were made in central and southern Germany.

From about 1600 Weight-driven brass-cased lantern clocks for hanging on the wall made in England.

The very first clocks merely struck a single note on a bell at the hour. One Gothic wall clock, claimed to be the earliest in existence, rattles a stone in a brass sphere, cowbell style. Clockmakers soon invented the count wheel (also called the locking plate) which made it possible to strike the correct number of blows to the hour. It was used on every striking clock before about 1670, when another system was invented, and on con-

24 Astronomical clock of the late 16th century made in Germany. The dial is marked I to XII twice and also 1 to 24, as was the German practice at the time.

Knobs at the hours enable the time to be felt in the dark. Astonomical indications are at the back.

siderable numbers after that date, particularly on American and less sophisticated European clocks, until past the middle of the 19th century. The count wheel has around its edge a series of slots at increasing distances apart relating to the number of blows to be struck. When the striking train is released, the count wheel is rotated and an arm above it moves up and drops at every blow. When it drops into a slot on the count wheel, the striking train is locked again.

Before about 1700, a pin on the great wheel (the toothed wheel on the barrel or fusee which rotated once in an hour) lifted a locking lever to release the striking train. If the clock was not showing correct time, the hand could not be moved, so either the clock had to be stopped until the correct time came round, or the escapement had to be released by a lever which lifted the verge out of engagement with the crown wheel, to let the clock run down quickly until the correct time was shown. It was stopped by holding up the weight or, in spring-driven clocks, by a brake on the crown wheel.

The single pin was superseded by a star wheel with twelve points fixed to the arbor that carried the hour hand, turning once in twelve hours. The wheel driving the hand was made friction tight, i.e. provided with a clutch, so that the hand could be turned without having to run down the clock.

The French invented another system in the first quarter of the 16th century whereby the striking train was released not by lifting a lever, but by letting it fall after it had been lifted. The first lift of this let-off lever released the striking train and allowed it to make a few turns before being held up again until final release. The preliminary short run of the train is called the 'warning'. It became commonplace after the beginning of the 18th century. It can be heard on most striking clocks a few minutes before the hour.

The hammer for the alarm was operated by a crown wheel and verge to which the hammer arm was attached in many early clocks and even in English lantern clocks of the 17th century. A series of pins on a wheel moving the tail of the hammer arm became the universal method of sounding the hours in sequence.

One of the major problems of the men who made the first spring clocks was to provide an even output of power from the mainspring, which not only started with extra force for a short time when fully wound, but ran down in a series of ever-diminishing power surges. A solution devised by German clockmakers was to limit the range of the spring by stopwork, gearing that prevented its being wound too tightly or running down too much. They also provided a cam rotated by the mainspring. Another spring pressed a small wheel on the rim of the cam, an arrangement known as a 'stackfreed'. This absorbed some power from the mainspring, but less and less as the spring ran down. It also tended to smooth out power surges, but it was never really satisfactory.

The French or Italians introduced a much better arrangement known as the 'fusee'–the name is French, meaning 'thread', but the first known drawings were by the Italian genius, Leonardo da Vinci, as early as 1490. It incorporated stopwork. The mainspring working a fusee is contained in a barrel, to which the outer end of the coiled spring is fastened. The inner end of the spring is fastened to a central arbor. When the spring barrel is in place between the clock plates, the arbor is fixed so that the barrel has to be turned to wind up the spring. The fusee itself is fixed to an arbor which runs in the clock plates above the barrel. It is a trumpet-shaped barrel, cut with a spiral groove on its surface. At the larger end is a toothed wheel. A gut line or fine chain is fastened to and wound round the run-down barrel; the other end of the line or chain is fastened to the larger-diameter end of the fusee.

Because of a ratchet arrangement, the fusee arbor can be wound backwards without affecting the clock. This action winds the line from the barrel on to the fusee at an ever-reducing diameter. It turns the barrel to wind the mainspring inside. After winding is completed, the whole system unwinds to drive the clock. The power of the spring drops off as it winds down and, to com-

30

25 A tabernacle clock from southern Germany dated about 1590–1600. The upper dial has a single hand showing hours. The lower dial indicates time on a 24-hour dial. The pendulum in the front was added after about 1660.

26 One of the elaborate table clocks made in southern Germany. It is dated about 1560 and was made in Nuremberg. Time in hours is indicated by the lower ring, and the figure on top points to the minutes.

27 Small vertical French table clock, only about eight inches tall, made about 1600 by N. Plantart, Abbeville. The movement is horizontal, with the going train and its verge at the top and the striking train at the bottom, although the dial is vertical.

pensate for this, the line works on an ever-increasing diameter of the fusee, so that the barrel turns faster. It forms a variable gearing to provide a constant power output. The spring barrel is pre-tensioned (called 'set-up') to avoid slackness in the line.

The fusee was so successful that it was enthusiastically adopted by English makers from their earliest days in the spring clock market from the 1660s to about 1920. It not only made English clocks (and watches) famous throughout the world in the 19th century, but led eventually to the decline of the English clock and watch industries because makers would not give it up for the cheaper 'going barrel' adopted by the French and others after the inventor of the clock pendulum had concluded that a fusee was unnecessary with a pendulum-controlled spring-driven clock.

English makers incorporated fusees in the striking and chiming trains of clocks also, so that intervals between notes did not become longer when the clock ran down. Because of this addiction to the fusee, English makers were not able to follow the French when they made small movements in drum-shaped containers, which gave enormous scope to the French casemakers of the later 18th and particularly the 19th century. Some English makers copied the French styles in an effort to keep in the market. Their clocks although typically French at first glance, can be spotted by the giveaway high winding holes necessary with a fusee movement.

The going barrel was simply the spring in a barrel without the fusee, but teeth were cut round one edge of the barrel to drive the clock train direct. When the spring ran down, instead of the barrel being wound up in the opposite direction, as in a fusee arrangement, the arbor to which the spring was attached was wound forwards. This meant that the barrel continued to go in a forwards direction. It provided its own maintaining power also; that is, the power to drive the clock was maintained while winding. A fusee needs a refined arrangement combined with it to provide maintaining power. The simple endless rope or chain used in 30-hour longcase clocks also provides its own maintaining power.

The first longcase clocks from about 1660 to 1675 with short bob pendulums about ten inches long had maintaining power to prevent them from stopping when the clock was wound. A few long pendulum clocks of top quality also had it. It was operated by pulling a cord attached to a lever which opened shutters over the winding holes, allowing the key to be inserted. The lever also pressed a spring-loaded bolt on to a tooth of a train wheel to keep the clock going, and this system is therefore known as 'bolt and shutter maintaining power'.

The next period begins with the pendulum revolution, which led to the longcase clock driven by weights and the English bracket clock driven by spring and fusee.

The middle period

The pendulum in England

28 A Dutch pendulum wall clock made by
Johannes van Ceulen in about 1675 after
the style of the first pendulum clock of all,
designed by Christiaan Huygens and made
by Salomon Coster in 1658.

29 The dial and side of one of the famous Orpheus drum-shaped table clocks of the 16th century, showing Orpheus charming the animals. Of nine known to exist, one is missing. This one belongs to J. Fremersdorf, the Swiss collector.

30 Very rare early 17th-century large chamber clock or audience clock used for timing interviews. It has a 24-hour dial and strikes at every *minute*, on four bells every

quarter of an hour, and at the hour. It has been converted to pendulum and was probably made by a Flemish clockmaker in England.

To time the passage of stars accurately, astronomers counted the swings of a weight suspended on a thread, because it was much more accurate than the clocks with balances available at the time. How to make a mechanism for keeping the pendulum swinging and counting the number of swings was not solved until the gifted Dutch astronomer, Christiaan Huygens, invented a practical
28 pendulum clock. After such a clock had been made to his design by a Dutch clockmaker, Salomon Coster, he published details of it in 1658.

Huygens hit upon the idea of making a domestic clock by setting a table clock movement on its side and, in effect, replacing the foliot by an arm (called the
11 'crutch') that engaged with a separately suspended short pendulum. He had discovered that if a pendulum swung in a wide arc–if it had a large amplitude–any change in amplitude would cause a big change in time-keeping. He called this 'circular error' and was therefore at pains to keep the amplitude small. The only effective way in which he could first think of doing so with a crown wheel and verge escapement was to interpose step-up gearing between the pendulum crutch and the verge. He, or Coster, soon got rid of the gearing and hung the pendulum from a double thread between two curved 'cheeks' which were supposed to eliminate circular

error. Huygen's oldest surviving clock is spring-driven and mounted in a small wooden case for hanging on the wall. His first design incorporated a weight drive operating through an endless cord that provided power while the clock was being wound, a system employed subsequently on almost every longcase clock designed to be wound daily and used today on every automatically wound turret clock.

By what might now be thought of as a brilliant example of industrial espionage, a clockmaker, Ahasuerus Fromanteel, working in London, got to hear of Huygens' dealings with Coster. He made an arrangement for his son John to work for Coster from September 1657 to May 1658 to learn how to make pendulum clocks. By November 1658, Ahasuerus Fromanteel was advertising as well as making pendulum clocks in England under an agreement with Coster, to whom Huygens had assigned rights.

Practical English makers soon simplified the original design to such an extent that the benefits seemed to have been lost; nevertheless very practical advantages remained, and the verge and crown wheel clock with 42 short bob pendulum remained in production in England for more than a century. The bob refers to the small pear-shaped pendulum weight threaded on to the bottom of the pendulum rod, which was itself about six inches long.

What the English makers did was to abandon the separate suspension of the pendulum and the arrangement of 'cycloidal cheeks' to eliminate circular error, so that the pendulum swung in a wide arc and suffered timekeeping changes; but the timekeeping was still much better than that of the balance wheel or foliot, and the pendulum was not very sensitive to the angle of the clock. The clock could be moved to another place and, although not so level, would still go. This seemed to be throwing away more advantages of Huygens' brilliance, but the loss was counterbalanced by the robustness of the simpler arrangement. In order to achieve reasonably good timekeeping from a pendulum attached rigidly to the verge, they had to replace the rear pivot of the verge and the hole in which it ran by a different kind of bearing with less friction, a knife edge oscillating in a shallow V-groove, like the bearing of a pair of scales for weighing. A ꓘ-shaped brass part kept the knife edge from jumping out. Continental makers retained an ordinary pivot in a hole.

The English version of the pendulum clock meant that the crown wheel had to be horizontal; that is, it had to run at right angles to the other wheels and therefore had to be driven by a contrate wheel, like the continental table clock. The arrangement had another advantage, that clocks previously controlled by foliot or balance could easily be converted to operation by short pendulum. The original crown wheel was replaced

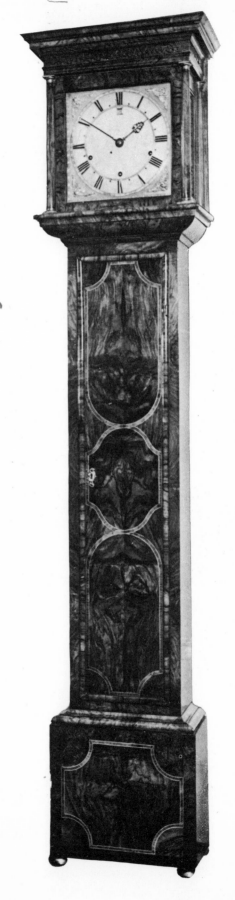

by a contrate wheel driving a pinion on a vertical staff, on the top end of which the crown wheel was now mounted. New holes were provided to take the verge horizontally and the pendulum fixed to one end of it.

Many conversions of existing clocks, particularly lantern clocks, were made, and they can be detected today by traces of the modifications that had to be carried out. As the lantern clock was held proud of the wall by its hoop and spurs, there was room for the pendulum to swing outside the back of the clock. In many continental countries, existing clocks of many kinds, wall clocks and table clocks, were also converted, often with the pendulum suspended over the front of the clock, so that it swung across the dial.

Naturally clockmakers began producing their lantern clocks with short pendulums hanging at the back, inside or outside or sometimes in the middle of the clock, or, on the continent, in front as well.

The pendulum changed the course of clockmaking history. It heralded the introduction of the longcase clock, a particularly English style, and an age of wooden cases generally, for which there was probably an economic reason. Continental clockmakers had to undertake long apprenticeships and to learn many ancillary skills connected with making metal cases for their clocks. The English maker had to compete. Plenty of cabinetmakers were available, so he called upon them to produce wooden cases for his metal movements. Unfortunately, we know very little about the casemakers of the 18th century because they did not sign their products.

Wooden cases had been used on occasions by continental clockmakers. The earliest in England were little 18,35 more than dust covers for some brass lantern clocks, which, instead of being suspended from a hook, were stood on a wooden bracket fastened to the wall. The idea may have originated in Holland where this type of wall clock persisted for many years after it had been abandoned in England.

When the pendulum clock arrived, English clockmakers designed a new case to go with it. In effect, they took the bracket and its hood off the wall and stood it on a long wooden trunk to enclose the weights, thus creating the longcase clock. The first longcase clocks were not very tall, about six feet, had small dials about eight inches across, and narrow trunks to their cases because there was no pendulum to swing in the trunk; the pendulum was a short one behind the clock movement. The early cases were veneered in ebony and of plain architectural style with classical triangular tops.

The spring-driven English clock, developed at the same time, was an almost exact counterpart of the longcase clock without its trunk and plinth at the bottom. It was supplied with a bracket for fixing to the wall, or was used without bracket and stood on a table. It is usually known as a bracket clock.

32 Ebonised 8-day striking longcase clock made by William Clement, London, about 1680. It is only six feet six inches high, like early longcase clocks of the time. It is one of the first with an anchor escapement and long pendulum, which Clement probably invented.

33 Elaborate floral marquetry case of a longcase clock by James Clowes of London, made about 1695.

34 The unusual decoration of this case is an inlay of pewter, brass and tortoiseshell in the manner of the French Boulle work. It is an English clock of 1690–95 by Daniel Quare, the Quaker clockmaker, and runs for a month at a winding.

35 A typical English country clock with a lantern-type movement, but in a wooden hood on a wall bracket. It has a long pendulum and alarm, and was made by Thomas Stripling of Lichfield about 1760.

Their longcase and bracket clocks made London makers famous in many parts of the world throughout the 18th century. After about half way through the century, thousands of makers outside London became most prolific and proficient in manufacture, so that the longcase clock became universally known and appreciated, while the London men concentrated on the spring-driven bracket clock.

32 About 1675, another major breakthrough occurred, when it was discovered how to apply a long pendulum efficiently to a clock. If a pendulum of about thirty-nine inches long were used with an ordinary verge and crown wheel escapement, it would have to swing in an arc two or three feet wide. It can be made to work with such an escapement and a much smaller amplitude—the French produced such clocks—but the arrangement was

not really satisfactory. Someone—the credit is given generally to an English clockmaker, William Clement, but it may have been the irascible scientist Robert Hooke —produced the simple solution of 'flattening' the crown wheel to make it just like any other flat wheel, but retaining its special saw teeth. Instead of having a verge, he designed a different form of staff with pallets, which was called an anchor, because it was shaped rather like 1 a ship's anchor. (It is often called a 'hook' on the continent, perhaps because of Hooke). The earliest dated longcase clock known was made by Knibb, however.

The anchor escapement and long pendulum meant that the pendulum's swing had much greater dominance over the rate of the clock and, as the amplitude of swing was relatively small, there was not so much variation in timekeeping through circular error as with the verge and crown wheel operating a short pendulum. For the first time it was possible to make clocks that would keep good time, as close as a minute a week. The escape wheel used with a long pendulum swinging from one side to the other in one second could easily be provided with thirty teeth so that it turned round once, with sixty jumps, every minute. In other words, a seconds hand could be fixed to the end of the escape wheel arbor.

The long pendulum was ideally suited to the longcase clock, which at once became the most accurate domestic clock of its time and the first to have a seconds hand as standard. To accommodate the swinging pendulum, the case had to be made wider. At the same time, it became taller to maintain an aesthetic proportion, and the dial became wider, to about ten inches. The date was about 1675. By 1700, clocks had become larger still, and soon the twelve-inch dial became generally established. Towards the end of that century, clocks with dials of fourteen inches were being made in some country areas.

The early architectural style was followed very quickly by a Jacobean pattern with twisted wooden pillars each side of the hood and with a flat instead of a triangular top. Carved cresting, an ornamental strip along the front of the flat top, was often applied. About 1700, the plain pillars returned and sometimes fluted ones were used. A domed top for the hood, at times with three metal ornaments, also became popular. Dials remained square until after the first quarter of the century, when the break-arch became increasingly common. It added a half circle to the top of the dial. The top of the case was also made break-arch in style, but not until a number of years later, from about 1760.

Another feature of earlier longcases was a glass or bull's-eye glass in the door in front of the pendulum, and a glass window each side of the hood so that the movement could be seen. Some clocks had pierced wooden or metal frets at each side of the hood, backed by coloured silk, to allow the striking to be heard. Nearly all longcase clocks struck the hours.

36 Dial of a longcase clock made by George Graham, London, between 1730 and 1740. Clocks at the time had to be set by a sundial, and the equation of time dial at the top, and equation hand on the time of day dial, showed how much ahead of or behind sundial time the clock should be at different times of the year in order to show correct clock time.

37 Provincial 8-day longcase clock by Edward Barlow of Oldham in an oak case of about 1750. It has a 'Halifax Moon' dial, a black face indicating new Moon and a white one full Moon.

Woods used tended to follow the trends of furniture after the first ebony veneer period. There was a short period of olive-wood cases before 1700. The wood was veneered to look like oyster shells, which resulted in beautiful and very valuable clocks. Burr walnut veneer was a favourite from about 1690 to 1760. Parquetry was introduced at about the same time. Veneers of different woods and colours were laid on the carcase of the case to form geometrical patterns, usually of fan and star shapes. The patterns became more and more elaborate and invaded the whole case instead of just the corners. All-over patterning, commonly representing foliage, flowers and birds, is called marquetry. It went out of fashion again, probably because of the increasing expense, about mid century, and the simpler parquetry came in again, revived by provincial makers.

Cases ornamented with Chinese scenes painted in lacquer on gesso, so that the patterns were raised, were introduced at about the same time as marquetry. Primary colours were generally favoured for the scenes on a black background, but a red ground, or one of buff, blue or green, was occasionally used. The lacquer fashion lasted longer than that of marquetry and enjoyed a smaller revival near the end of the century.

Mahogany was one of the most exciting new woods for furniture in the 1720s. By 1750 it had ousted walnut for all more important clocks and was taken up enthusiastically by clockmakers outside London for their better productions through the latter half of the 18th century and nearly half way through the 19th. Oak cases were made at all times for lower cost productions or for working clocks, intended, for example, for astronomers. The carcase of the veneered case was usually of oak, and pollard oak itself was occasionally used for veneering.

The dials and hands of longcase clocks followed a definite sequence and give a valuable guide to the age and authenticity of the clock. In general, the smaller the dial, the older the clock. A similar rule of thumb applies to cases: the smaller the case of an 8-day clock and the longer the door in the case, the older the case. Dials were of brass, with a silvered chapter ring having engraved Roman hour numerals and Arabic minute figures. The narrower the chapter ring, the older the clock. Minute numerals were at first engraved between two engraved circles round the dial, then outside the engraved circle with the minute divisions. They became bigger and bigger until they disappeared after the mid 18th century, so that the smaller the minute numerals, the older the clock. The quarter-hour divisions on the inner side of the chapter ring were usually missing on clocks made after 1750. Ornaments in the corners (or 'spandrels') of the dials were at first very simple, showing winged cherub's heads. Then they became floral.

38 Lacquered case on a black ground of a clock by Christopher Gould, London, made about 1695. All the minutes are numbered, a feature of early long pendulum clocks.

39 The longcase clocks illustrated so far have movements that run for a week or more, but large numbers were made that had to be wound daily. Some were

Hands were of blued steel, the minute one a pointer and the hour one elaborately carved and pierced. They too changed with time, and different patterns were favoured by different early makers. In the 18th century they were considerably standardised, being supplied by specialist hand-makers. Painted dials on an iron sheet began to supersede brass ones from about the last quarter of the century, and simpler matching hands— hands of the same pattern, but one being bigger than the other—were introduced to combat rising costs.

In the later 18th century and through the first half of the 19th, more and more 'makers' bought movements for longcase and bracket clocks from embryo clock factories in Birmingham and London, and had them supplied with their names already engraved or painted on the dials and even engraved on the clock plates.

Other indications not infrequently appear on longcase clock dials. A calendar is so common that it can be regarded as standard. Moon dials, showing the age of the Moon, are quite common. Less common are tidal dials showing local times of tides, animated scenes, and the equation of time, which indicates how fast or slow the clock should be compared with time indicated on a sundial.

Longcase clocks that run for about 30 hours at a winding and intended to be wound daily have been made exceptionally well made, like this 30-hour movement by William Dent of the early 18th century. It has a verge escapement and short pendulum.

40 Mahogany longcase clock by Thomas Walker, of Newcastle, made about 1770, with a Moon dial in the arch. Around the Moon dial is another indicating local tidal times. The third hand on the main dial indicates the date.

since, or almost since, the first longcase clock appeared. They have as genuine a heritage as the 8-day version, but have been for some reason despised by clock collectors. 30-hour clocks were made by the famous London clockmakers of the 17th century and after about 1700 were made in tens of thousands in many parts of the country.

The best early London-made 30-hour examples had plated movements and were wound by a key. The going and striking trains were side by side, but with the going train on the left, in contrast to its being on the right in a standard 8-day clock. Early provincially made clocks were directly descended from the lantern clock with posted-frame movements, sometimes with iron corner posts. The layout generally followed that of the lantern clock, with the striking train behind the going train.

Almost all 30-hour longcase clocks have a single weight to drive the hands and sound the hours. The weight hangs from a Huygens endless rope or chain and in most cases is wound by pulling on the appropriate length of rope or chain. Rope was earliest and continued to be used by country makers until about 1780, although many ropes have since been replaced by chain. Pulley wheels intended for chain have identifiable chain grooves cast in them.

Some posted-frame movements in 30-hour longcase

clocks even retained the loop and spurs on the back so that they could be hung on a nail on the wall as a lantern clock, or on a hook in the case, in contrast to standing on the shelf, known as the seatboard, in the clock case. Northern makers quickly followed the London lead by employing plated movements, which eventually became universal. A northern posted-frame longcase clock seems to be unknown.

39   30-hour longcase clocks often have a single hand to show the hours, with brass dials, spandrels and separate chapter rings like their 8-day counterparts, the only difference being the absence of minute divisions around the outer edge of the chapter ring. Many were later converted to two hands. There are also clocks made with two hands, and with seconds hand, calendar, and even Moon dial, again like their more expensive brothers. In general, however, painted dials were used for 30-hour clocks after about 1790.

Cases were usually locally made and therefore appear in enormous variety, sometimes well proportioned and at others very ungainly. They were nearly always made of oak until after the turn of the 19th century, when deal was used and grained with 'scrumble' to imitate oak or mahogany. Such clocks are now sometimes seen in furniture shops stripped of paint and sold with other deal furniture as 'pine'.

30-hour longcase clocks were smaller in stature than most 8-day clocks and had square dials because the break-arch shape increases height. They were intended for cottage use, where headroom was almost invariably slight, for which reason they are generally called 'cottage clocks'. An oddity of these longcase clocks is that the 'seconds' pendulum does not always swing from one side to the other in a second. A seconds pendulum was probably unimportant because the escape wheel turned anti-clockwise, and a seconds dial could not be fitted.

44   The spring-driven bracket clock took a different course from the weight-driven longcase clock, although some features of the dials and hands remained in step with fashion. During the first period from about 1660 to 1700, when the clock looked like the removed top of a longcase clock, the bracket clock case had pillars at the sides, either plain or with barleysugar twists. The first big step in the general standardisation was to eliminate the pillars, leaving a plain square case with glass front and square brass dial behind it. The top of the case was domed and was surmounted by a carrying handle. The size varied from about fourteen to thirty inches high. The dial had a silvered chapter ring and in the corners were gilded spandrels, like longcase clocks. Hands were made of blued or almost black steel.

41   Before about 1760, most bracket clock cases were black. Normally the case was made of oak and veneered with ebony, but a variety of other woods was also used and dyed black. A few early bracket clocks were veneered

44 One of the earliest shapes of the English bracket clock was architectural, like this bracket clock of about 1665 by Edward East, London, with a seven-inch dial. The movement had eight pillars and was converted to rack striking, perhaps by East, and then to anchor escapement, when one pillar was removed.

About 1750 another major change was introduced, which made a slow start but eventually engulfed almost all clocks. It was the round glass, following the shape of **43** the circular dial. The earliest glass was flat and fitted into a square door on the front of the clock. Every bracket clock made during the first half of the century had a front door. The circular glass began to alter that, as clockmakers found it simpler to fit the glass into a circular frame, called a 'bezel', which was hinged like a door. Glasses – and dials – soon became domed, improving the appearance of the clock. The exception was the long-case clock. Those with round dials are rare.

It was becoming expensive to make dials of six pieces – the dial plate itself, which had to be cast and hammered out flat, then polished and matted to give it a textured surface before gilding; the chapter ring, which had to be made in the same way, have feet fitted, and then be polished and engraved with the rings and chapters, and finally silvered; plus four corner spandrels that had to be cast, cleaned up and gilded.

Dial-making was undoubtedly one of the bigger costs in producing any clock. Some of the work would be given to specialists or 'bought-in'. The pressure to cut costs is evident from an examination of earlier and later clocks of this period, or at any other. For example, look closely at the spandrels of an English clock of the late 17th century. They will have been not only cleaned up after casting, but finely chased, that is, gone over with chasing and burnishing tools to remove casting roughness and to polish the larger surfaces. Gilding afterwards always produced better results. Then look at the corner spandrels of a normal clock made around or after mid 18th century. The spandrels will be more elaborate, but the casting will have been left rough and hardly touched or not touched at all before gilding.

The first circular dials eliminated the separate chapter ring, and the dial plate itself was engraved with the hours and other indications. The dial plate was silvered all over. No spandrels were needed because there were no corners. Thus the parts were reduced to one and the number of operations in making the dial cut to less than a quarter.

The next step was to eliminate the cost of engraving and filling dials. The first painted ones for bracket clocks appeared after 1750, and they gradually increased in popularity as the century proceeded, black Roman numerals on a white ground being most universal. **48** French clocks of the time had the better black on white enamel for their chapters, but there were difficulties in enamelling large surfaces, so a large enamelled dial is rare. The French avoided the problem by making separate pieces for each chapter.

The bracket clock continued to be fitted with the quite primitive but convenient bob pendulum and verge **42** escapement. This arrangement has a quite distinctive

with walnut and very few with olive wood. These normally command higher prices because they are unusual. A few cases were veneered with kingwood and some with tortoiseshell; occasionally a case was made in **45** marquetry or lacquered with Chinese motifs, but the numbers of black cases swamped all the rest.

The first major change in the shape of the dial and case came in the second quarter of the 18th century, **46** when the break-arch was introduced. The extra space in the semicircle was occupied by one or more subsidiary dials, such as a 'Strike/Silent' for turning off the striking, or a 'Rise and Fall', for regulating the timekeeping by altering the length of the pendulum without moving the clock to open the back. There were usually numbers round this dial. Bracket clocks did not have seconds hands except very rarely.

The change in shape of the dial was accompanied by **45** a change in the shape of the case. Either it became taller and the opening in the front followed the break-arch contour of the dial, or the case itself was made with a break-arch top, to follow the shape of the dial and glass. This did not mean the disappearance of the square dial; it persisted, but in smaller and smaller numbers as the century continued. Before mid 18th century, the break-arch became by far the most popular style.

tick-tock which indicates that the clock is going. Some makers of earlier clocks liked to reinforce the indication visually by attaching a short 'mock pendulum' to the front end of the verge, the pendulum being attached to the back end. The mock pendulum, which could be seen swinging in a slot in the dial under XII, was also a useful levelling indicator.

The flat, circular and slightly domed pendulum bob, known as the lenticular pendulum, was introduced in the 17th century by the most famous English maker of all time, Thomas Tompion, but did not become general for bracket clocks until quite late in the 18th century. Tompion reverted to Huygens' principle of suspending the pendulum separately. He used a strip of spring steel instead of a thread, a system that every clockmaker copied eventually. The thread persisted in France longer than anywhere else. It could be wound up or down to adjust timekeeping.

A number of verge and bob pendulum clocks were converted to anchor escapement with short lenticular pendulum. When a mock pendulum was incorporated it lost the attraction of its swing of 40 degrees or more, looking rather inadequate with the short arc of the anchor movement. Some converters removed the mock pendulum, unfortunately, which looks even worse.

English bracket clocks usually strike the hours on a bell on top of the clock inside the case. To enable the bell to be heard, the sides of the case were normally open, but covered with silk attached to a metal fret—a plate with decorative piercing. The most common type of piercing after mid century was fishtail. The number of clocks with this feature is surprisingly large.

Some very early English clocks struck a single note at the half hour also, but they are uncommon. A half hour note is a continental feature and it would be unusual to find a French striking clock that did not sound the half hours. With all early striking systems which had count wheels to sound the correct number of hours, it is possible for the time indicated to become out of phase with the blows struck. Some time about 1670, a parson-clockmaker, Edward Barlow, invented a new system that prevented a clock from striking incorrectly, and which had the additional advantage of allowing the strike to be operated at any time to repeat the last hour it had struck.

For their more expensive productions, clockmakers began to incorporate this rack striking, arranged so that it could also be operated by a thin cord through the side of the clock. Pull the cord when the clock showed, say, half past eleven, and it would strike eleven. Repeaters were a luxury for bedroom use, when obtaining a light involved sparking tinder to ignite a candle to see the clock.

Early repeaters usually chimed the quarters as well as the hours, a higher bell note sounding after the hour,

48

46 Bracket clock with a break-arch dial by Daniel Quare, who worked in London from 1671 to 1724. It has a calendar dial in the arch, and the quarters and hours are made to repeat on five bells by pulling a cord at the side.

47 Movement of the Daniel Quare clock, with a finely engraved backplate, bob pendulum and pierced back cock at the top.

one for a quarter past, two for half past and three for three-quarters past the hour. In the 18th century, some elaborate bracket clock movements were made that repeated the hours, quarters and half quarters, so that the owner could judge the time shown by the clock to the nearest seven and a half minutes. The finest repeated the hours, quarters and minutes.

Bracket clocks were also made from the early days with chiming mechanisms. A chime by definition sounds on more than one bell. The earliest version, which has a history almost as long as clocks themselves, is called the ting-tang, after its sound. It comprises two bells, the first giving a higher note than the other. At the first quarter the clock chimes *ting-tang*, at the half hour *ting-tang ting-tang*, at the three quarters three *ting-tangs* and at the hour four of them before the hour bell, which starts on the hour as shown by the hands.

47 Chimes for bracket clocks were made with three, four and more bells up to eight, which usually ran through the musical scale as a chime. Chiming tunes is a

late feature. If a clock has Westminster chimes, it was 54,59 made in the 19th or 20th century. The Westminster clock itself, called 'Big Ben', was not installed until 1858. Its chime was called Cambridge chimes before then because it was based on a melody from Handel's *Messiah* and first installed in a Cambridge church.

Musical clocks playing on bells were made from about the mid 16th century, but not frequently. A musical clock differs from a chiming clock usually by having another mechanism, wound separately, in addition to the striking and chiming, but musical chimes would entitle a clock to be called a musical clock. Although 49 bells were most commonly the source of the music, organ clocks were made from before 1600, and also flute clocks. A number of celebrated composers of the 18th century were pleased to write special melodies for the mechanical music of clocks.

Lower priced versions of the earlier repeater bracket clock were made in some numbers in the first part of the 19th century, repeating only the hour, like the

51 A bracket clock with a round dial but full-sized door holding the glass. It has an anchor escapement and lenticular pendulum. A pull cord at the side winds a separate spring causing the hour strike to be repeated. Thwaites & Reed were the makers about 1820, although another name is engraved on the back plate.

52 French Boulle clock with its original bracket, made about 1725. The case has a tortoiseshell veneer inlaid with brass, and the legs and ornaments are of ormolu.

53 Fine balloon clock by J. Barnard, who was apprenticed in 1793 to Thomas Udall, and later worked at St John Street, Clerkenwell, London, according to the Worshipful Company of Clockmakers' register of apprentices.

earliest versions of the finer London clocks. They are still to be found and are an attractive purchase. They have traditional mahogany or ebonised cases and round dials usually with fishtail side frets. The top is often of break-arch form and always with a carrying handle. The movement has an anchor escapement with short lenticular pendulum. Many different names of the supposed makers appear on the dials and back plates, seen through a glass door at the back.

Many bracket clocks of the 19th century came from embryo factories and were engraved with a 'maker's' name to order. That is why so many are, on examination, found to be more or less identical. It accounts, too, for the prevalence of the fishtail fret. In fact, the name

'bracket clock' even for many early versions is a misnomer too. Those with glazed rear doors and engraved back plates were clearly not intended to be stood on a bracket. They were table or mantel clocks.

After about 1760, several new shapes began to challenge the traditional table or bracket clock. One of these was a reversion to a much earlier period, the Gothic. The Gothic shape in wood, however, was architectural, like a lancet window, and indeed the shape is usually called the 'lancet'. Other shapes were the pagoda top and the flat top. The biggest change was the balloon, an idea that originated in France.

Although earlier makers sometimes produced a small clock as a *tour de force*, most productions were between

51

54 Mahogany inlaid with brass is used for the case of this striking and chiming clock by Hill Bros. of Teignmouth. It is dated about 1870 and has alternative chimes, one the Westminster, introduced about twelve years earlier.

fourteen and thirty inches high. The new shapes were also fairly large by modern standards because they were generally in scale with the rooms of the period. The new styles, made during the Regency period, are lumped together as Regency clocks. They had striking or chiming movements and were also made as timepieces only, unlike most earlier clocks. The movement was sturdy and usually without ornamentation, or with only a small amount. The pendulum was lenticular with spring suspension and anchor escapement, and the clock spring-driven through a fusee, so the timekeeping was good.

Regency clocks departed from the almost universal black case that had become traditional in table clocks, being made commonly in mahogany but also in walnut and other woods, following the fashion for furniture at the time.

It should be obvious from what has been written in this chapter that English clocks during the 18th century were very much standardised in type if not so much in production. Thomas Tompion, at the end of the 17th century, had already begun to use batch production methods. At the end of the longcase and bracket clock periods in the later 19th century, clock movements were nearly all made in factories, although today they appear to be and are often claimed to be hand-made by individual craftsmen.

Some longcase clocks were, however, nearly always made individually and were for a number of years neglected by collectors. They are the precision clocks known 60 as regulators. Early ones, such as some made by George Graham, who first specialised in precision timekeeping in England, were much like the longcase clocks of the time. To avoid too much backlash (clockmakers call it 'shake') of the hands, giving incorrect readings, and to reduce friction and increase precision, the clocks were simple timekeepers with no additional work to do, such as striking a bell, and the hands were not concentric but indicated on separate dials for hours, minutes and seconds. Pendulums were compensated, to avoid the effects of temperature changes lengthening and shortening them, by using a jar of mercury for the bob, after Graham, a series of rods of different metals, after Harrison, or some other compensation, one of the simplest forms being a wooden rod sealed against moisture with varnish.

A regulator was almost always housed in a plain wooden case with a glass door and had an all-over silvered dial. Some cases were of oak, but most later ones were of mahogany. Some were made for hanging on the wall. Clockmakers themselves used regulators to regulate the timepieces they made or repaired and often designed and constructed their own regulators, perhaps as a masterpiece after apprenticeship, but some makers and, later in the 19th century, some firms, such as Dent, 55 Barraud & Sons, Barraud & Lund, and J. Smith, made them for sale to others.

One long-pendulum English clock of the 18th century was a wall clock, but for special use as a public clock. As it was particularly favoured by tavernkeepers it is usually known as a 'tavern clock'. Another name is 58 'Act of Parliament clock', because when a tax was placed on the ownership of clocks and watches from 1797 to 1798, the local tavernkeepers, it is said, rivalled each other by using attractive clocks to entice customers. The tavern clock has a very large dial of from two to three feet across, without a glass and with brass hands, usually of spade form. The dial is circular, hexagonal or a modified form of these shapes. The colour is usually black with gold designs, though occasionally a lacquered one is seen. The movement is a timepiece without strike and is normally tapered towards the top. There is an anchor escapement and seconds pendulum with a weight, usually of brick shape, to drive the clock. Tavern clocks, also called 'coaching clocks', although more strictly these are the large clock-watches hung inside coaches,

56 2-day marine chronometer for ship's navigation by Parkinson & Frodsham of London, made about 1830. The brass-bound mahogany case holds the movement in gimbals so that the dial remains level when the ship is heeled over. An up-and-down dial shows the hours left before rewinding is necessary.

57 Heavy ormolu French clock of about 1850 with a twelve-piece enamelled dial. Later enamelled dials had thirteen pieces fitted together to make a circular dial. Then it became possible to enamel large one-piece dials.

58 Tavern clock with a lacquered case, made about 1775. It has a long pendulum and is weight-driven. The dial is over two feet in diameter. These timepieces are also called 'Act of Parliament clocks'.

59 Mahogany bracket clock of about 1900 with small control dials giving chime silencing, adjustment of the pendulum, and alternative chimes on eight bells, or Westminster, which is on four bells. The hands have reverted to a Gothic style, and the case ornaments reflect an earlier period.

60 Fine regulator in the classical mahogany case, but without a glass door through which the pendulum may be seen. The aperture in the dial shows the hours, the large hand the minutes and the smaller, counterbalanced one the seconds. It is marked 'Shelton' on the back cock (from which the pendulum is suspended), and the month movement, dated about 1760, is identical to one by George Graham.

were in fact made from the early part of the 18th century.

The true coach, coaching or travelling clocks were up to about five inches in diameter and looked like very large watches in decorative cases. They struck the hours, and many 18th-century ones were also repeaters. They can be recognised by the joint in the pendant allowing the clock to hang flat from a hook against a vertical surface. They were made from the 17th century until the beginning of the 19th and followed watch styles in general. Late ones were in fact verge watch movements fitted into circular wooden frames. These are called 'sedan clocks' by antique dealers, although they were known as 'post chaise clocks' when they were made.

Another specialist clock for travelling, a precision instrument, unlike the travelling clock, was the marine chronometer, made in some numbers in England from about 1780 until the First World War. It is an exceptionally beautiful instrument, always enclosed in a brass case because it was intended for navigating at sea. The brass case is held in gimbals in a cubic mahogany box so that the chronometer remained level when the sailing ship was tacking. There are two main types, the 8-day version normally intended for shore stations and the 2-day for navigation at sea. The two English makers who founded the industry were Thomas Earnshaw and John Arnold, fierce rivals in business. They made chronometers in quantity after John Harrison had, twenty years earlier, proved that timekeepers could perform accurately at sea. They were followed by many other makers whose names became well known in precision timekeeping. From time to time the Royal Greenwich Observatory sells off surplus chronometers, but it is only in recent years that their true value in collector's terms has been realised, except, perhaps in America, which bought many of the earlier marine chronometers offered for sale. Earnshaw and Arnold each made about a thousand chronometers, but, although a marine chronometer is very rarely destroyed, try to find one of them today! Those by other makers are not difficult to acquire.

There is one more English clock of the period that became an international design. It is known simply as the 'English dial', because it appeared to be just a framed dial. The first versions were made at the beginning of the 19th century. They were wall clocks a foot or more across with spring and fusee movements, some time-pieces and some striking as well. The wooden frame was normally circular or octagonal, sometimes decorated with fluting, or brass or ivory inlays. Hands were almost invariably of spade form. Other versions had a small box below the dial to accommodate a longer pendulum and are known as 'drop dials'. Later ones were intended for offices or railway premises, and were well made.

The German Black Forest industry made dial clocks in large numbers also.

56

The middle period

The pendulum in Holland, France, Germany, and the United States

61 German Telleruhr or plate clock of about 1740 for hanging on the wall. It has a verge escapement and a cow's tail pendulum over the dial. The crown wheel is on an arbor that extends from the side of the movement.

and then, after disappearing for a century and a half, turned up in North America disguised as the weight-driven shelf clock.

In Holland, there was interest in the longcase clock developed in England; in fact, some writers on horology believe that the longcase originated in Holland. The Dutch followed the English style quite faithfully, but became fond of a wavy minute circle engraved on the dial. They also modified the case for some clocks, bowing the front and sides of the plinth (the base of the case), and introducing large claw feet and large ornaments, such as eagles, on the top of the hood.

The Burgundians and the Flemings were perhaps the first mechanical clockmakers, and the Dutch were making weight-driven frame clocks from an early time. One form, the Zaanse, made in the Zaandam area, 62 encased in wood instead of sheets of iron with coloured designs painted on them, was the common clock in Huygens' time and was still being made a century later.

In the farming area of Friesland from about 1700 to well into the 19th century, Dutchmen constructed a particular kind of bracket clock driven by a weight. It was heavily ornamented by cast lead frets at the top and sides of the posted-frame movement. The bracket itself was of wood, also heavily ornamental, with a small roof or hood at the top over the clock. It was called a 'stoelklok', meaning a stool clock. The short pendulum, separately suspended, was not operated through a crutch, but by an arm from the verge which would 63 normally have been one arm of a foliot, thus avoiding replanting of the crown wheel to a horizontal position, as in English bracket clocks. Huygens had devised this simple arrangement while experimenting with long pendulums on turret clocks, for which it was also used in Holland. The stoelklok struck a blow at the half hours as well as the full hours, a common continental practice.

Stoelklok frets were usually gilded and coloured, and the dial was coloured with paint as well. The Dutch continued to paint dials throughout their clockmaking history, even while the English and French were following Huygens' lead of a separate metal chapter ring. In England, the brass dial had become universal and it was not until after 1750 or so that the painted dial began to enjoy some popularity. The Dutch, being meticulous and neat in everything they do, had their clock dials repainted regularly, when they became dirty and worn—there were artists who specialised in dials—whereas it seemed to be a matter of principle with the English to retain the 'original' painting however flaked and battered or worn it had become. Dutch makers even provided paper dials to stick over worn painted ones during the 19th century, although today Dutch collectors heartily dislike restored dials!

Some Dutch makers followed English bracket clock styles in the 18th century, however, the ebony-veneered

It would be difficult to overestimate the influence of Huygens and the clocks made under licence from him by Coster on the future of clock industries in all countries. There were other men striving to design practical pendulum clocks, but the Dutchman's was the only one with a truly scientific basis and although his ideas were not at first adopted, they gradually came to be absorbed over many years.

The Huygen's pendulum clock was fitted into a rectangular wooden case that hung on the wall or could be stood up. The dial had a velvet ground, reminiscent of Victorian framed dried flowers. The wall clock never attracted the attention of the public who bought clocks in England at the time (wall clocks in Britain, called 'English dials', belong to a later period), but the Huygens' style was popular in Holland, where it was known as a 'Haage klokje' (a Hague clock), was followed in France,

64 One of a pair of ceramic vase clocks made in France by one of the Bovet family in the first half of the 19th century. The Bovets worked in Fleurier and were famous for their very ornamental watch movements. This clock has a fine movement with centre seconds hand.

65 Mantel clock by Gille L'Aîné, Paris, in a Meissen case set in ormolu showing Scaramouche and Columbine modelled by J. J. Kaendler. Factory records of 1744 describe this piece as one of the most difficult pastoral groups completed.

66 Wooden movement of a late 19th century German Black Forest dial type of clock in an octagonal frame. The wheels are of brass. Earlier versions had wheels of wood.

cases and brass dials being slavish copies. The dial ornaments were almost identical, as well as the hands, mock pendulum, broken arch features, where incorporated, carrying handle and case top ornaments; but if any painting was involved, the difference was readily noticeable. Some Dutch bracket clocks had typically Dutch painted Moon dials in the break-arches. The Moon dial was uncommon on English bracket clocks, but not on both English and Dutch longcase clocks. The English Moon dial was painted, but in a different style from the Dutch.

The typically Dutch stoelklok was followed by another typical production, the staartklok, also from Friesland, at the beginning of the 19th century. The word means 'tail clock'. It was a throwback in design, because the movement was still a posted-frame, and an unwary collector could date one as much as a century before its time. It was controlled by long pendulum and anchor escapement. It was a wall clock with a narrow case below the hood (the tail) to enclose the pendulum, but not the single, often ornamental, weight, which hung outside in front. An ornamental 'window' disclosed the pendulum bob. The staartklok had a removable hood like a longcase clock, sometimes with ornaments on the top, and the dial was painted and invariably was of broken arch shape, sometimes incorporating in the arch animated figures of a rocking ship, operated by the pendulum, or a Moon dial. Some small staartkloks were made at

the time, but are very rare now. The Dutch frequently hang a kind of sampler, a strip of embroidered material, over the curved top of the hood.

Although production had finished by the last quarter of the 19th century, staartkloks and other traditional styles are still turned out today in Holland with German movements and two weights. They are called 'English clocks' in Holland! Indentification of them is not difficult.

The French are one of the oldest if not the oldest clock-producing country and greeted the advent of the pendulum clock by copying it fairly closely and calling it a 'religieuse' clock because of its severe style and dark colours. The French religieuse clock soon acquired some of the characteristics of the English table clock of the time (the so-called bracket clock), and despite its name was often ornate by English standards. These early pendulum clocks were typical of the Louis XIV period, the first fifteen years of the 18th century, but for some strange and confusing reason are often known in France as Louis XIII clocks, which was the period before the invention of the pendulum clock! The front of a later religieuse clock had pillars which, combined with the domed top, were supposed to represent the front of a palace, the glass in the door having an arched top. The dial also departed from the original simple chapter ring on a velvet ground, which was replaced in some models by twelve shaped pieces in white enamel with black

67 French ormolu cartel wall clock signed by the Parisian maker Denis Masson, who became a master clockmaker in 1746. The asymmetrical case in ormolu is set off by piercing backed with red silk.

68 Magnificent French longcase clock in Boulle marquetry of brass and tortoiseshell, surmounted by a figure of Father Time. It was made in the Louis XIV period, about 1700.

69 French Directoire period striking clock in a cut crystal vase with ormolu mounts, made about 1795.

Roman numerals on them, and a gilt repoussé (embossed) metal 'zone', as the centre of the dial is called.

The most typical French clock of the Louis XV period (1723–1774) was the so-called balloon shape, which stood on a bracket on the wall. It was developed from a less waisted shape that appeared in France earlier in the century and had a surge of popularity long after its introduction because the shape was reminiscent of the hot air balloon experimented with by the Montgolfier brothers in the later 18th century. The balloon shape had its imitators in England, but in a very plain wooden form. The ornamental French style was copied in Switzerland–in fact, it was adopted by the Swiss, who called it the 'Neuchâteloise clock' and who still make large numbers in a derived style today.

The early French versions were very decorative. Some were made with Boulle marquetry cases, inlaid with 53 metal and tortoiseshell. More often the case was in bronze, or of vernis Martin, carved oak treated with a varnish imitating oriental lacquer to give it a metallic appearance, invented by the Martin brothers in about 1730. The oak carving was veneered with pearwood and filled with a preparation to hide all the joints. Colours were applied if required and the final glossy finish obtained by a number of coats of varnish, which after a period of time became covered by a network of small cracks.

Vernis Martin was also commonly used as an alter-

70 Japanese clock of the early 1800s which is attractively decorated and lacquered but is primitive horologically as it still has one hand, and a verge and foliot, which was superseded in Europe a century earlier. One foliot weight can be seen under the front of the bell.

piece dials. They became known as 'cartel clocks', for a reason that is not clear (the word means 'challenge', and also 'cartel', in the English sense). Some other countries copied the cartel style, notably Sweden.

Also in the Louis XV period, a form of longcase clock came into favour, but it was very different from the English version, being Rococo in style. In fact it was a spring-driven bracket clock, standing on a pedestal. After 1700 a true longcase clock in the same style was **68** introduced. The long pendulum's action could be seen through an ornate window in the elaborate violin-shaped trunk. The French did not like the anchor or recoil escapement of the English, having developed an escapement of their own, known as the pin wheel, that gave a good performance and needed only a small arc of pendulum.

Some of the longcase clocks were regulators, in much the same style, but with centre seconds hands and extra fine movements. Many had the improved dead-beat escapement, an accurate version of the anchor escapement, invented by an Englishman, George Graham, partner of and successor to Thomas Tompion.

For their spring-driven clocks, the French used a going barrel, and usually a frame with circular back and front plates. As the dial was circular, they were able to make the movement small enough to fit behind the dial, while the English were still making rectangular movements of much larger size, mainly because of the fusee drive which dictated the dimensions. The more or less standardised size and shape of the French movement gave the case designers much more scope. All they had to do was to leave a drum-shaped opening for the whole **65** of the mechanical part of the clock including the dial. At a later stage, the movements were enclosed in drums, and called 'drum movements', so that they could be fitted as a single component—what is today referred to as a 'module'. This applied to pendulum-controlled movements as well as the more portable balance wheel and hairspring versions of several countries in the 19th and 20th centuries.

Casemakers therefore became more important in France than in other countries, where their names are usually still unknown. After 1850 in France, casemakers were obliged by law to mark their names on cases. The reign of Louis XVI, from 1750 to 1790, was the age of the casemaker, a time of extremely ornamental clocks in huge variety. The sculptural clock with classical figures, animals, vases and columns became very popular. A clock carried on the back of an animal was a common theme.

The pillar clock, comprising four pillars supporting a **72** drum-shaped clock below which hung a short pendulum with a sunburst bob, was introduced. It became very popular later. The lyre-shaped clock appeared; it was to have a big influence on American styles in the 19th

67 native to bronze for the ornate wall clocks that appeared during the reign of Louis XV. The dials were round. The design of the case was often based on curling acanthus leaves and usually, but not always, asymmetrical. The earlier twelve enamelled pieces forming the chapter ring were superseded by thirteen separate pieces shaped to fit together into a complete circular dial. This was necessary before methods of firing the enamels on larger surfaces were discovered in the mid 18th century. The wall clocks generally had one-piece dials, but a few earlier ones were fitted with thirteen-

century. The forerunner of the carriage clock can also be discerned among the prolific output of the Louis XVI period. Another departure was a break-away from the disc-shaped dial and a reversion, in the vase clock, to the very early ball clock of the 16th century with a band dial. The rim of the vase had the hours marked round it and rotated once in twelve hours. The time was shown by a pointer over the front of the moving rim. Some clocks had a second rim indicating the minutes.

Longcase clocks were still made in the same shapes, but the ornamentation was in many cases not as florid. Regulators appeared in the more restrained English style, for it was a time also of technical advances and the more formal case design accorded more with the precision of the timekeeper, but large enamelled dials, by then perfected, were fitted in contrast to the English silvered dial.

The clocks of the period most commonly seen today are lumped together under the generic name of 'ormolu', which means 'ground gold' and refers to the fact that the bronze sculptural cases were fire-gilded by applying powdered gold amalgamated with mercury, which was heated to evaporate the mercury (a process that resulted in the death by poisonous fumes of some of the gilders).

The ormolu, being thick and finely finished, was of a high quality by later standards. Prices today are high and almost impossible to judge with any degree of accuracy by horological standards. Such clocks have been reproduced ever since they were first made, in all levels of quality. Most seen in shops today are inferior reproductions made in zinc alloy castings, which are very expensive to repair if damaged.

All bronze cases gilded before about 1850 were treated by the ormolu method and have a fine green-gold colour. Over-enthusiastic cleaning has removed much of the gilding on many clocks that survive. On others the gilding has blackened and can be restored by treatment with a cyanide restoring solution (which is also highly poisonous). Fire-gilding is not practised today except perhaps by one specialist workshop, which handles the fire-gilding of special pieces of hand-made silver, so a badly worn ormolu piece would have to be electroplated, a process that gradually replaced fire-gilding after about 1870.

The French Revolution from 1792 to 1795 brought a halt to most horological activities, some clockmakers removing themselves from the scene, including the most celebrated Abraham-Louis Breguet, who returned for a

72 Four-pillar French clock from the rear, showing the Harrison gridiron pendulum that compensates for temperature differences that could affect timekeeping.

73 French provincial hanging clock with an inverted verge escapement at the bottom of the movement. Like many continental public clocks, it strikes the hour, then

repeats the notes after two minutes. Such clocks were made in the Franche-Comté area from about 1750 to this century.

time to his native Switzerland. The Directoire period that followed immediately, and lasted until 1799, brought renewed activity, but with some restraints and a wave of enthusiasm for Egyptian motifs following Napoleon's campaign in Egypt. There were attempts to introduce decimal timekeeping, with ten months to the year and ten hours to the day. A few clocks were made that kept and indicated decimal time. They are almost impossible to get hold of now. One of the most significant styles of clock for England appeared – the skeletonised clock under a glass dome. The French version was a delicate piece of mechanism compared with its later English descendant.

The Empire period in France from 1800 to 1830 coincided with the Regency period in England. Both brought more restraints but still a strong influence from Egypt, with sphinxes, scarabs, Isis lion's heads, eagles, palms, winged globes, claw feet, beading, swans, laurel bands, and so on. The clock on four pillars with pendulum in the centre seems to have been most popular. Some had pendulum rods made up of a row of bars, imitating the temperature compensation invented by John Harrison in England. Vase-shaped clocks were made with orthodox dials, and ormolu clocks incorporating classical figures remained popular.

The finest clocks of all from a horological viewpoint were made during the Empire period. They were of a superb standard of craftsmanship, of high precision, represented exceptional technical insight, and had a classical elegance of design that borrowed little from earlier periods. The names of makers of that time are well known to discriminating collectors: A.-L. Breguet, Ferdinand Berthoud, Pierre Le Roy, Jean André Lepaute, Antide Janvier, and M. Raingo are among them. Anyone visiting Paris should see some of their works at the Arts et Métiers museum, near the Metro station of that name.

64,

75 Fine English fusee mantel clock on carriage clock lines by E. Dent, 82 Strand, London, who made it between 1840 and 1850. The firm later made the Westminster clock called 'Big Ben'.

76 French four-glass clock (with four glass sides but larger than a carriage clock). It has a visible Brocot escapement on the dial and a mercury pendulum. Such clocks were made in England and France from about 1850 into the 20th century.

Their clocks still come up for auction and, although inclined to be highly priced, are still better value than some of the more popular sales purchases.

After mid century came what is known as the Second Empire period, from 1852 to 1870. During it, huge numbers of earlier styles of clock were reproduced by zinc casting methods, fitted with standardised drum movements. They are the commonplace French ormolu clocks of today. It was also a period when industrial methods were applied to what formerly were luxuries, and many of the other clocks of the Second Empire period and the years that followed to the end of the century represent an interesting period to today's collector of limited means, although despised by collectors of a few years ago. Many books stopped at the end of the Empire period. The clocks concerned are a by-product of the French Industrial Revolution and include the later marble clock period, which had begun in First Empire times, again probably through the influence of the east Mediterranean campaigns. Cases were made of marbles of different colours and it was also discovered how to make multicoloured cases from fragments of different coloured marbles cemented together.

Clocks were made in Besançon from the 17th century; later the town became well known for carriage clocks,

but today it is most famous for watches. Main provincial clock production was in the region of Morbier–Morez–Foncine, where the Comtoise clock was invented. The Comtoise movement is different from any other and was so successful that during the 18th century it gradually replaced the different types of movement produced in other provincial areas of France.

French provincial clocks are very much less sophisti- 73 cated than those from Paris and were ignored almost entirely in Britain as unworthy of buying until recent years. Most are longcase clocks in rather ungainly locally made cases, either straight-sided or violin-shaped. The pendulum is uncommonly ornate, being rather like a huge bob instead of a rod with a bob on the end. In fact it is made of two parts of embossed sheet metal, varying in width from about four to ten inches, often decoratively coloured, but usually just gilt.

The movement has a frame, like the lantern clock, with posts at the corners and straps between the top and bottom iron plates. There is a horizontal crown wheel driven by a contrate wheel, but the teeth of the crown wheel point downwards, with the verge underneath it. The striking is effected by a toothed rack attached to a sliding rod. The arrangement provides no warning in the horological sense, but does give one in the lay sense, because after an hour is struck, two minutes later the striking is repeated.

Morbier movements of the traditional pattern were made until the First World War, but later ones have an anchor escapement instead of the crown wheel. They are commonly found on the continent without a case. The movement is provided with an oval break-arch or repoussé brass background to a circular enamel dial and is hung on the wall, with the elaborate pendulum and two driving weights below. Morbier clocks can still be found in continental street markets, particularly in Holland, but most probably they are recently made.

The earliest German clock industries were in the towns of Augsburg and Nuremberg in the south and, 77 when their influence declined in the late 17th century, another area made rapid progress with a quite different form of clock. It was the Black Forest region in Baden and Württemberg, which, without knowledge of the sophisticated metal productions of the old centres, began making simple wooden clocks from about the middle of the 17th century. Despite the forest, it was a farming area. The farmers could do little but look after their stock in sheds during the cold winter snows, and developed their own craft of woodcarving. It is surmised that someone brought to the area a simple wooden clock made elsewhere and that this was copied by the Black Forest farmer-carvers and developed by them into the traditional Black Forest product. It is likely that metal clocks were also made in the area.

The movement itself was made of <u>wood</u>, even to the

77 Early wall clock from south Germany with simple iron pillar frame held together by wedges. Made in the late 17th century, it has one hand, an alarm setting disc in the centre, a painted iron dial and a 'cow's tail' pendulum over it.

78 Black Forest organ clock with automata representing a theatre scene in the painted wooden dial. The figures strike bells, and the clock plays eight tunes on forty-four pipes on the hour and on demand. The organ is operated by a pin barrel.

79 French carriage clocks were made in many versions. The double one has a barometer on one side with compass on the top. The other is unusual for its painted battle scenes, recalling the pendule d'officier. Both were made in the early 20th century.

80 German trumpeter clock of about 1780 in a hand-carved Black Forest case. At the hour, double doors at the bottom open and two trumpeters inside blow their horns.

81 Austrian wooden clock bearing the date 1687 and signed 'IW'. Behind the 8½-inch wooden dial is a wooden pillar frame with wooden wheels. Originally the clock had a balance wheel, but has been converted to short pendulum with the verge. Even the hand is wooden.

wheels mounted between two vertical posts united at top and bottom by cross-pieces. It had a single hand and was weight-driven. A foliot controlled it through a simple pin wheel instead of a crown wheel. Reproductions are made today by Swiss and German firms. Later, four-poster frames were used, with beechwood top and bottom plates, corner posts and straps in which brass bushes were inserted to take the pivots of the wheels. The beechwood did not come from the Forest. The foliot persisted until nearly halfway through the 18th century, and the verge escapement itself until the first quarter of the 19th, but it was used then with a short pendulum that hung in front of the dial and was known as a 'cow's tail'.

Brass wheels were introduced in the late 18th century, but still with wooden arbors that had steel wire pivots in the ends. The dials were wooden, at first with painted zone, numerals and decoration, until hand-coloured paper pasted on the wood became more practical for production. The decorative paper dial was finished with a varnish glaze. Most dials were of break-arch shape. The movement, enclosed in a case made of firwood from the Black Forest, and fronted by the larger dial, would

be fastened to the wall so that its long pendulum (introduced about half way through the 18th century) and weights on chains hung below it.

Black Forest makers at first ignored striking and only began to make striking clocks in the first part of the 18th century; shortly after that one of them, Anton Ketterer, had the strange idea of designing a clock that imitated the cuckoo as a 'chime' before striking. It was not an immediate success but nearly half a century later someone used the same bellows and pipe mechanism operated by wires in a carved wooden clock imitating a chalet, and the cuckoo clock became famous all over the world as a novelty. Earlier cuckoo clocks had standard cases.

From its early days, the Black Forest industry had great success in exporting. Travelling salesmen–sometimes the clockmakers themselves–carried clocks on their backs on a special frame, replenishing them daily from the main stock, which they had transported by cart to a central point. These salesmen, in their knee-breeches and wide brimmed hats with their Tragstuhls on their backs, were also the subject of some clockmakers, who carved them in wood, about eighteen inches high, holding a small spring-driven working clock in front.

82 American wagon-spring shelf clock in a typical steeple case. A leaf spring in the base provides the power. The glass front panels are painted in verre églomisé style.

83 American clocks were underrated by the British collector for some years, because they were made in the 19th century and because the movement was made of 'rolled brass and wire'. Americans obviously appreciated them, and they are now recognised as being good examples of early mass-production methods. This one is a shelf clock by Seth Thomas, made about 1840 in Thomaston, Connecticut. The weights that drive the striking and going sides are suspended at each side of the case. The pendulum controls an underslung anchor escapement.

The carving was coloured. Good reproductions of these are also made today.

The dial type of Black Forest clocks sometimes had automata in an opening in the break-arch, often two small carved wooden men striking the bell at the hours. These clocks, with or without automata, are still called 'Dutch clocks' at times in England because they were originally imported by travelling salesmen who referred to them as 'Deutsch [German] clocks'. Oddly, they are called 'Swiss clocks' in France. The British and American public believe that the German cuckoo clock is Swiss.

The era of the wooden clock movement came to an end when the Americans started making brass clocks by machine at prices that undermined the Black Forest trade, which for nearly 200 years had depended upon outworkers specialising on different parts of the clock at workbenches in their own homes. A Black Forest straw hat manufacturer, Erhardt Junghans, responded by setting up a factory on the American system, which was followed by a number of others. Their earlier productions, from the later 19th century, are now coming into antique shops. One traditional style of clock, the postman's alarm, continued in production on traditional lines, but with an alarm instead of striking work. It was a wall clock with a circular framed dial, like the English dial, but was weight-driven with the weight and pendulum hanging below it. Some had open faces and others a glass with the hour numbers painted on the reverse of the glass. The alarm was set by a central boss.

84 A London dealer's workshop. It is not easy to find a dealer with such expert facilities of his own. Aubrey Brocklehurst, London.

85 American lyre clock, a form of <u>banjo</u> <u>clock</u> made in the first quarter of the 19th century.

The <u>American industry</u> was founded by immigrant clockmakers, mainly from England, who established quite extensive clockmaking regions centred on Boston and on Philadelphia. Longcase clocks were more common than bracket clocks because springs were difficult to obtain. The typical American longcase clock is rather like the English provincial clock of the 1750s, with a swan-neck crested top to the hood. Makers depended upon imports for the metals they needed and, when the Declaration of Independence in 1776 caused their supplies to be cut off, they had to turn to wood, following the pattern of the Black Forest makers over a century earlier. The Americans, however, devised semi-mass-production methods of manufacturing wooden clocks at prices that no other country could match with any type of clock.

The first factory was operated by a water mill and was set up by Eli Terry, who had an order for 4,000 longcase clock movements to be made in wood and delivered in three years. It took him a year to invent the machinery and set up the factory, but he completed the order on time, and made a profit, which was not usual in those times of great change. He sold the factory to two young clockmakers with whom he had working partnerships, one of them named Seth Thomas, who was largely instrumental in developing and popularising for the mass market what is now regarded as the typical American shelf clock.

A shelf clock is usually two to three feet high in a rectangular wooden case, rather like a much larger version of the original Huygens' pendulum clock. Early versions had wooden movements. The shelf clock was driven by rectangular weights hanging in the sides of the cases from pulleys in the top corners and controlled by a pendulum and anchor escapement working underneath the escape wheel. In the 1840s, the factory-made brass movement was introduced and within a very short time had superseded the wooden one.

Cases at first were delicate with small feet and cresting on top, but in the 1830s a heavy style with half pillars at the sides was introduced. This was itself ousted from about 1845 by a simpler form with a picture frame type of surround, known as ogee or 'OG'. Another popular shape was the steeple shelf clock, with conical wooden spires at each side of the inverted V-shaped top. The Americans developed a form of wooden cased wall clock or shelf clock seemingly based on the French lyre clock shape. Called a 'banjo clock', it has a drum-shaped top and rectangular base with a narrow tapered trunk between them. A similar clock with a circular base is called a 'girandole clock'. It has been suggested that the styles owe their influence to Swedish clockmakers who had emigrated to North America, because they have a resemblance to Swedish house clocks and have Arabic instead of Roman numerals, in the Swedish style.

An attractive feature of earlier shelf clocks is the decorated glass in the door, covering the dial and the pendulum, which is reverse painted (see page 10) with patterns, flowers or scenes.

The strangest American clock was in one or other of the traditional shapes, usually shelf form, but was driven by spring instead of weight. As coiled springs were difficult to obtain and make, a waggon spring, like the leaf spring in the suspension of a vintage car, was mounted in the base of the case. Its ends were 'wound' upwards and they pulled down to drive the clock. Thousands were made, but have been so much sought by collectors that they are very difficult to come by today.

Other early clockmaking countries include Italy, Austria, Sweden, Switzerland, and also Japan which produced some original and fascinating timepieces.

The later period

Novelty, special and early factory clocks

86 An unusual moving arm clock featuring
an Indian dancer in an ultramarine enamel
niche. The arms move upwards to show
hours and minutes, then drop to the
bottom. Probably French.

87 Late 19th-century clock with a French Brocot visible escapement movement sold by an English company in India. In the left support is a barometer and in the right a calendar giving the month, day and date, and also the equation of time (the difference between clock and sundial time).

88 Typical English skeleton clock in architectural style with fusee and pendulum. It is a timepiece (i.e. without strike) and would normally be under a glass shade (dome), but many struck once at the hour. Large numbers were made from 1860 to 1880.

The most simple and quite common form of skeleton clock struck a single blow on a bell at each hour and is known as a 'one at the hour' clock. There are others with various degrees of complication – some going for a month, even a year; others with striking, chiming or musical movements; versions with almost every kind of escapement and controller known. Almost invariably they had fusees. A skeleton clock without one is probably French. The skeleton clock period was from 1820 to 1900, but reproductions almost impossible to tell from originals (except that the price is sometimes higher!) are being made today. Also there are 'makers' converting old fusee movements with tapered plates into skeleton clocks.

English fusee clocks of other types were still being produced after 1900. The movements were undoubtedly of higher quality than those from foreign sources, which adds to their collector-value today. As recently as 1970, dial clocks with fine English fusee movements were being sold in large numbers in the London street market in Leather Lane for £4 each. They even had their original cranked keys with them.

Very, very occasionally it is possible to unearth a memorandum clock in an antique shop. They were made in England in the latter part of the 19th century in oak cases for table or mantle with a single architectural top. The top is hinged at one side, and raising it discloses a brass drum on top of the clock movement with some small ivory tickets in a pocket at the side. In the drum are radial slots for every quarter of an hour. A reminder is written on a ticket which is placed in the slot representing the time to be reminded. At that time, the clock delivers the ticket to a small trap under the dial and at the same time rings an electric bell operated from a battery in the base. The movement of the clock was a standard English fusee with pendulum.

A French clock especially favoured by the Victorians was the black marble mantel clock, especially that with a visible escapement. An incidental advantage of the heavy case was that it was rarely shifted when dusting, so that the timekeeping of the short pendulum was not disturbed. The visible escapement in front of the dial under XII is a form of anchor known as the Brocot, after its inventor, working with a small escape wheel. The acting faces of the anchor are small pins of red stone. Brocot clocks were made from about 1850 up to the First World War, but later ones have not been regarded with any favour by collectors until now, unless incorporating a Brocot perpetual calendar on extra dials. Some of the more attractive Brocot clocks had 'four-glass cases', the brass frame having glass sides all round.

The French clock that has escalated most in price in recent times is probably the carriage clock, in a brass case with a handle on top, and front, back, sides and top of bevelled glass, so that the highly finished movement

There are, of course, no distinct periods of single hand-made, batch-made and factory-made clocks, because they merged into each other. When a new method was introduced, there were always makers who continued on traditional lines because they resisted the inevitable 'lessening of quality'. In the second half of the 19th century and the first quarter of the 20th, a large variety of clocks was being produced by many methods; moreover, 'French' clocks were being made in England and America, 'Viennese' and 'French' clocks in Germany, and 'English' clocks in Holland, as well as domestic productions.

The conservatism of most clockmakers in England during the Industrial Revolution in Victorian times gave foreign firms an opportunity to invade the English market, so that an increasing number of French clocks, German clocks and suddenly, in 1842, American clocks were seen. English makers reacted by taking a French idea, modifying it and producing it in tens of thousands. It was the skeleton clock, the brass frame of which was decoratively pierced and often represented a famous building or monument. The clock had no case, but was displayed under a glass dome, known as a shade, in the same way as the stuffed birds in dried grasses and flowers admired by the Victorians.

There were very few makers of skeleton clocks, with the consequence that there are a number of recognisable patterns. Some of the frames have decorative scroll or bar patterns, but others were supposed to represent cathedrals and famous buildings such as Westminster abbey, Lichfield cathedral, York minster, the Scott Memorial in Edinburgh, and the Royal Pavilion at Brighton. It is rare to find one bearing the maker's name.

89 *left* Pendule d'officier decorated with army symbols. The French carriage clock developed from earlier pendules d'officiers. This one is a grande sonnerie, sounding quarters and hours every quarter of an hour, is a repeater, and has a pull alarm (wound by a pull cord). It is 12½ inches high and was made by Courvoisier & Compe with fusee and verge in the late 19th century. *centre* Austrian brass clock of the 18th century with mock pendulum, going trains, short pendulum and verge escapement, with original travelling case. *right* German gilt metal pendule d'officier by Johann Mainz (1753–1826) with pull alarm and repeat.

can be seen. To make it portable, it is spring-driven and has a platform escapement; that is, a platform across the top of the plates holding an escapement controlled by a balance and spring, which is not affected by movement like a pendulum.

90   Early carriage clocks have always commanded high prices because of their excellence of quality and often richness of case. They were usually originally sold with an extra leather-covered wooden outer case for transport. The carriage clocks seen in shops today are almost invariably factory-made. The usual form of escapement of such clocks is the cylinder or horizontal, which can be recognised because the edge of the escape wheel, which moves in tiny jumps, intersects the staff of the oscillating balance wheel. Many carriage clocks have had the cylinder escapement replaced by a lever, in which there is a lever between the escape wheel and balance wheel. This has the advantage of improving the timekeeping and also making the clock repairable. Clockmakers generally will not repair cylinder escapements today. But at some time in the future, such clocks will be regarded as converted, like the early lantern clock converted to pendulum.

French carriage clocks were made in Besançon, near 79 the Swiss border, at St Nicholas d'Aliermont, near Dieppe, and in Paris, where the earliest makers were. At later times, makers in Paris finished the clocks, after having bought the parts from one of the other two manufacturing centres. All types of carriage clock were made – simple timepieces, alarms (recognisable from the small dial below the main one), strikes (which sound a single note at the half hours as well as the hours), hour repeaters (which sound the last hour at will by pressing a knob on top of the case), minute repeaters, and even grande sonnerie (sounding the full hours after every quarter is struck). The Austrians also made high quality carriage clocks in the earlier 19th century, and there were a few English makers of high quality pieces. Carriage clocks are still made today but mostly by German firms. They can be identified by their lightweight movements.

The Industrial Revolution in France, later than that in Britain, created an especial interest in industrial machines and mechanical novelties, which inspired clock designers to associate clocks with working models of steam beam engines or captains steering rolling ships, and there 93 were lighthouse clocks, railway engine clocks, and even 92

90 Carriage clock with a centre seconds hand, alarm (indicated on the lower dial), and repeater (operated by the button on top). It was made by Japy Frères, pioneers of factory production.

91 Unusual French carriage clock in the form of a sedan chair, made in the late 19th century. It is eleven inches high.

clocks shaped like submarines. Among the most interesting were the mystery clocks. One of them has a figure of a woman in Grecian dress placed on top of the clock and a separate pendulum suspended from her hand. The pendulum, once started, continues to swing and control the clock. These clocks, made in the 1870s are, when working well, surprisingly accurate. The secret is that the figure stands on a platform that is linked to the escapement of the clock. As the pendulum is swung, it causes the figure to rotate slightly in the opposite direction (action and reaction being equal and opposite). The rotation of the figure releases the clock escapement, which twists the figure in the opposite direction, and the cycle is repeated. The rotation of the figure is so very small (about 0·4 mm) that it is almost impossible to detect even if staring at the figure from a short distance.

Another mystery clock had a floating hand, which pointed to the time, but had no apparent means of turning it. The hand is actually attached to a circular sheet of glass, which is sandwiched between two other sheets of glass. It has a toothed edge and is turned by a toothed wheel driven by a shaft from a clock movement in the base of the case.

One mystery clock, invented centuries ago, is occasionally seen in later forms made in this century or the latter part of the 19th. It comprises a shallow bowl, around the rim of which are the hour numerals. The bowl is filled with water and a special floating 'tortoise' put in the water. The tortoise (it should be a turtle, but the clock is traditionally called a 'tortoise clock') swims to the correct time and continues to creep around the edge to indicate the time. The secret is that a clock movement in the base of the bowl rotates a magnetic hour hand under the edge, and the tortoise, containing some soft iron, follows it.

The mystery clock that appears most often for sale was made in fairly large numbers in France around the 1880s. A figure, usually a Grecian woman holding out an arm, or an elephant holding out its trunk, supports a pendulum with a clock dial surmounting it. The clock and pendulum are in one piece and suspended a short distance above the centre of gravity. Once this is wound and set swinging, it will continue to swing and keep time until it runs down. The secret is that the pendulum movement releases the escapement, which causes a small weight to move in the opposite direction from the

of the 20th century because the public was intrigued by the new ticket issuing machines of the time. They were made in large numbers by French and German makers 94 during a few years before 1914. Time is shown by a 'book of tablets', the pages of one being turned every minute and the pages of the other every hour, to show the time in digits. Digital clocks enjoyed a new wave of popularity in the 1970s. It is a cycle that repeats itself over periods of years since the first digital clocks appeared in the 16th century.

An American was responsible in 1883 for a strange clock now known as a 'flying pendulum clock', which is fascinating to watch but a hopeless timekeeper. On the top of the case of a French version was a cherub with an umbrella, from the edge of which hung a thread with a ball on the end. At each side stood a thin wire post. The clock movement turned the umbrella, the ball flew outwards on its thread, and the thread twisted round a post and stopped the umbrella. The thread then unwound and the cycle was repeated with the other post. Many are seen today without the cherub and umbrella; they are German reproductions currently being produced.

The most-remembered Austrian clock is the Vienna regulator, a wall clock of high quality and precision. The large and heavy brass-covered bob of the seconds pendulum could be seen through a glass fronted and sided case of mahogany veneer with inlay and carving at the bottom. True Vienna regulators are not often seen, but the German industry copied the regulator in huge quantities.

The German 'Vienna regulators' were cheap pendulum clocks much smaller than the originals, with light pendulum bobs, but they kept good time for domestic use. A peculiarity of many is that they have a seconds dial and hand, but the hand goes round the sixty minute divisions in about three-quarters of a minute—so the term 'regulator' is ludicrous! Nevertheless, such clocks are gradually finding their ways into antique furniture shops.

From about 1880, the Germans introduced a clock that ran for a year at a winding. Year clocks had been made from the early 18th century—there is a particularly famous year bracket clock by Thomas Tompion—but as special pieces. By using a torsion pendulum, the Germans could make such clocks in quantity. The clock was under a glass dome, and below the movement hung a ball or cylinder which wound round very slowly in one direction and then in the other. After about 1900, the pendulum was changed to an assembly of four balls. These are usually called '400-day clocks' in Britain and 'anniversary clocks' in the USA. They are still made in large numbers, but the earliest versions, particularly some in cases imitating lighthouses, and others with skeleton movements, are always interesting to the collector.

pendulum and keep it swinging (action and reaction again).

86 Animated clocks were made in some numbers in France and Germany from about 1800 to the last quarter of the century. They were a revival of the animated clocks made in the ancient clockmaking centre of Augsberg in the 16th and 17th centuries. All kinds of automata were employed at so many activities that it would be impossible to list them here.

Animated three-dimensional scenes under a glass dome included a clock in a church tower or elsewhere. One favourite was a ship tossing on a stormy sea. The clock mechanism operated levers under a fabric painted with waves, which gave a very realistic impression of a dangerous swell while a sailing ship pitched and yawed on it.

The Americans invented ticket clocks at the beginning

the other, being hung from a suspension spring and a helical balance spring. The height is twenty-five inches.

93 The back of a late 19th-century beam engine clock by Sutton. The beam is the controlling balance of the clock, being held by crossed suspension springs. The 'piston rods' just dangle in the 'cylinders'.

94 Ticket clock made in France about 1920 under an American patent of 1902. Today similar clocks are very popular under the name of digital clocks.

A group of clocks to which little attention has been paid are the first electric domestic clocks. Rare now is the Bain clock, made before the mid 19th century, operated by an earth battery. It was in a long case and the pendulum was kept swinging by an electromagnet operated by cotton-covered wires from a crude battery in the garden, comprising a quantity of coke and some zinc plates (or some copper and zinc rods), that had to be watered in dry weather!

The French were perhaps the first to market electric clocks in any numbers with their Bulle model, under a rectangular glass cover. The pendulum was a coil of wire swinging round a curved bar magnet, and the Leclanché cell was contained in a brass cylinder holding the clock movement. The Swiss Telegraph Manufacturing Co. made a much better timekeeper called the Hipp clock, recognisable by a small free-swinging toggle attached to the pendulum rod near the top. From time to time it depressed a contact to impulse the pendulum only when the amplitude dropped, which doubled the life of the cell.

Another electric clock first appeared on the market in 1909, the Eureka, driven by a battery in the base. It has a very large balance wheel and spring, mounted with the plane of the wheel vertical and dominating the clock. In the 1930s, the Americans came along with the Tiffany Never-wind electric clock, superficially rather like the German 400-day torsion pendulum clock under a glass dome.

A device worth looking out for was also a product of the Industrial Revolution, when timekeeping at the factory became an important factor in many people's lives. It is a stand for a pocket watch that converted it to an alarm. The pocket watch had to have a fusee that turned as the watch ran down and would operate the alarm on the stand.

Industrial clocks, apart from the first watchman's clocks made in the 19th century in England and Germany, have received scant attention from collectors. The first watchman's clock was in a tall case of oak or hung on the wall and had a rotating dial without hands. Around the dial was a series of oak pegs that could not be reached. The watchman visiting the place where the clock was situated, pressed a lever which depressed a peg indicating the time of his visit.

Early time recorders marking a paper tape with a time, and early time-switches, are worth consideration. Early time-switches were gas controllers, clock movements that incorporated a gas tap to turn on and off gas-lit street lamps. They were first used by a builder, John Gunning, in Bournemouth because he could not sell his houses in unlit streets. After the Road Traffic Act of 1934, time recorders were made, and used for a time, to show how long a lorry had been driven. There must be some still to be found.

Postscript
Taking a clock home

95 Front plate of a miniature timepiece
by Thomas Tompion. It has a lenticular
pendulum at the front, adjustable by
removing the foot of the case. It repeats
the hour by one to six blows on one or
two bells, on the cord being pulled.
There is also an alarm. Fitzwilliam
Museum, Cambridge.

A specialist dealer will sometimes set up a clock for the new owner. Once this service was not exceptional, but today few dealers have the staff to spare. In any case, the new collector should be interested enough to learn how to carry home and set up the clock himself.

90 Some clocks–carriage clocks, for example–were intended for carrying and with them no problem arises. Other spring-driven clocks with balance wheel control can be transported without special preparation, although they were not intended for use as travelling clocks. Clocks with spring drive and short pendulum can be moved short distances if carried upright and carefully so that the pendulum does not swing sharply enough to damage its suspension or escapement. (A 'short distance' is across a room or from one room to another.)

45 English bracket clocks have a carrying handle on top, but it is very unwise to lift the clock by the handle alone today because the case will probably have weakened, especially if it has been kept in a centrally heated room. Always support the clock from underneath with one hand.

If a spring-driven pendulum clock is to be carried any distance, the pendulum must be secured or removed. Some clocks have a hook or a clamp on the back plate for this purpose. The pendulum of an English verge movement is not removable, and a hook is often provided 42 under which the pendulum rod can be sprung.

Any loose parts should be removed and carried or packed separately. This applies in particular to weight-driven clocks. The weights must be unhooked first of all. If there are more than one, stick labels on them to indicate the sides from which they were taken. Some weights are heavier for striking and chiming than for timekeeping. It is best, but not essential, for the clock to be run down when this is done. The gut or other lines will then be wound off the barrels and can be fastened where they will not tangle with any other clock parts.

It is also best, but not essential, for the springs of a spring-driven clock to be run down. Never, in any circumstances, try to let down a clock spring by levering up the 'click' (the ratchet) that keeps it wound, or by dismantling a wound clock. It is highly dangerous. A suddenly released spring is lethal: it can smash and propel part of a clock wheel with the force of a bullet. Even clockmakers have been maimed and on a few occasions killed by a moment's carelessness when letting down a spring. There is a safe way of letting down a spring which is best learnt from someone who can do it.

To remove a pendulum is simple if care is taken. Most pendulums have a short suspension spring attached to the top. The spring terminates in a folded strip of brass with a steel pin through it. This cross pin sits in a groove in the pendulum cock, a projection at the top of the back

plate. If the pendulum rod is grasped, lifted slightly and then moved away from the back of the clock, the suspension spring should become unhitched. Often it is better to lift the pin out of its groove with one hand while gently raising the pendulum with the other.

In French clocks the suspension spring is usually fastened at the top, and there is a cross pin through its lower end on to which the pendulum hooks. The pendulum is quite easy to remove. Earlier French clocks have silk or thread suspension in which the pendulum is hooked to a loop of fine thread. Many German Black Forest clocks also have pendulums hooked on, but to a metal loop. These too are easily removed.

The pendulum rod passes through a slot in the short arm at the back of the clock known as the crutch (unless the escapement happens to be an English verge). The slot may be open ended or closed and care must be taken in withdrawing the pendulum from it otherwise the escapement may be damaged. It is not necessary to remove the pendulum bob, unless it is hooked on to the rod, as in the case of a few clocks. If the clock has been regulated, it will keep good time in its new home if the bob is not interfered with. To carry a pendulum safely, attach it with some sticky tape to a strip of wood stronger than the rod, making sure that the suspension spring is protected.

Longcase clocks present a few extra difficulties in transport. The hood must be removed and carried separately, even if it is the type that locks. Most hoods slide forwards for removal, but earlier ones on shorter clocks slide upwards (and are known as 'rising hoods'). The movement will be mounted on a seatboard, a horizontal board across the top of the trunk. Sometimes seatboards are nailed in place; often they are not, and there is a danger of the movement and seatboard falling forwards when the pendulum and weights are removed. So watch this point. Obviously the movement and the seatboard to which it is fastened should be transported separately if the seatboard is not fastened firmly to the case. Even if it is fastened, make sure that it will not come adrift during removal.

When carting a longcase movement–or for that matter any pendulum movement out of its case–pay special attention to protection of the hands and the crutch at the back. It is not uncommon to find the bottom loop of a crutch or a hand broken off by having caught on something when handled carelessly.

Precision clocks need extra care because they are made more accurately with less tolerance in their parts, which are also more delicate. Weight-driven regulators 60 normally have extra heavy pendulum bobs. If a wooden rod is used, this is especially vulnerable because it will snap if carried horizontally without support for the bob.

When the pendulum is removed from a spring-driven clock, the clock will often begin to run down quickly and may strike or chime while being transported. To prevent this, and any damage to moving parts constricted by packing, make a wedge of newspaper or, better still, tissue paper and press it between the crutch and back plate just tightly enough to prevent the crutch from moving.

56 A marine chronometer is a precision instrument that is spring-driven and has a balance wheel and spring. Although it is designed for service while travelling in a ship, it still needs protection when being carried any distance. Before the chronometer is locked in its gimbals by the lever provided, the balance wheel should be wedged. The chronometer balance wheel is especially heavy and is not shock-protected like the balance wheel of a modern watch. Therefore, to reduce the risk of bent or broken pivots, make two tissue wedges to be placed under the balance opposite each other.

Mercury pendulums are found in some regulators and French domestic clocks. They are for temperature compensation; as the rod expands downwards in hot weather, so the mercury in a jar or jars that comprise the bob expands upwards to compensate, and the pendulum remains at the same effective length. Jars of mercury should be transported separately. A jar is of glass or metal with a metal or glass cover. The amount of mercury is carefully calculated to compensate for the expansion of its chamber, as well as for the length of the pendulum rod, and any split will destroy the precision of the clock. Some mercury chambers are sealed and therefore easy to transport. Those on French domestic clocks are normally sealed, and some are more decorative than useful as temperature compensation.

Before the clock is set up again, have a look at the movement to see if it is very dirty or is worn. (This should really be done before the clock was purchased— but one always finds something not noticed at the time.) Clocks will run for scores of years and often for centuries if they are cleaned and oiled from time to time and, most of all, if dust is kept out of the oil. Before the Industrial Revolution in the 19th century, Britain's skies were blue more often than they are now, there was much less dust and many fewer corrosive chemicals in the air. Clocks had a good chance of survival for centuries without much wear. Today polluted moisture in the air gathers dust containing particles of quartz which are harder than steel. The moisture, condensing on a clock movement, turns the lubricating oil into a grinding paste in the bearings. The brass bearing holes usually wear oval because pressure between the teeth of engaging wheels and pinions tends to force them apart.

The correct way of dealing with worn pivot holes is to get a clockmaker to bush them, i.e. to drill them out larger and to press in fresh discs of brass with the correct-sized pivot holes drilled in them. A pivot hole will sometimes be found ringed or partly ringed by a series of crude punch marks. This is the work of the botcher, who has tried to squeeze the worn pivot hole back to its original size. It is considered fair practice by some clockmakers, however, to perform the operation with a correctly sized ring punch, which forms a groove round the treated hole.

A dirty movement can be cleaned, after removing the pendulum, by brushing it all over with a solvent such as carbon tetrachloride (sold by most dispensing chemists) or petrol, using a stiff brush and doing the job out of doors because of the fumes (and away from naked flames if petrol is used). Dry the clock very thoroughly afterwards to remove any deposits that may form and cause oil to spread. Clocks with balance and spring or other delicate parts must not be so treated unless the parts are removed.

A clockmaker would not clean a good clock in the manner described or clean it fully assembled. He would use an ultrasonic cleaner or, if a traditional craftsman, would scrub parts in a solution of soft soap and ammonia, wash them afterwards in benzine, and dry them with chalk or boxwood sawdust. Some movements exposed to view, such as in carriage and skeleton clocks, and the engraved backplates of English bracket clocks, are highly polished and lacquered after cleaning. Marine chronometer movements will usually have been 'spotted' and lacquered by the maker although they will not be exposed to view.

Dials that are painted white or in colour can be cleaned by removing grime and old lacquer with pure soap (a shaving stick will do) and water. The work must be done very gently as old paint has a tendency to lift. Finish off with clean water and a dry cloth and protect the clean dial by transparent lacquer. Enamel is much tougher than paint and can be cleaned in the same way. It is not lacquered afterwards.

Brass dials need only be washed in water containing some liquid detergent. Finish in clean water or a sticky surface may be left to trap dust. A separate chapter ring may be brassy because it has lost its original silvered finish. Re-silvering is a job for the specialist, although a skilled amateur could do it. There are still professional dial restorers in London's Clerkenwell. If any of the black wax is missing from the numerals in engraved brass dials, it can be replaced by black sealing wax. Remove and heat the chapter ring from underneath enough to melt some chips of wax placed on the surface. More details are given in practical books. Black enamel paint is an alternative material for filling numerals on less valuable clocks.

Wooden cases can be cleaned by normal methods explained in books on antique furniture. A good furniture polish is all that is necessary if the case is in good condition. If any parts are broken and can be glued in place, or it is necessary to glue in support blocks for strength, do not use one of the modern synthetic glues, such as impact or two-part types. It may be necessary to separate the joint at some future date without ruining that part of the case. Veneers often lift if the clock has been in a centrally heated house for any time. How to deal with them needs the advice of a furniture restorer. Anyone attempting to stick a piece of veneer in place should heed the warning just given about glues.

74   French marble clocks, popular in Victorian times, have returned to fashion today. Many were black and have become dull and greyish. They can be restored by polishing them with a thin paste of beeswax in natural turpentine, after cleaning the case with turpentine. The paste has to be rubbed hard, when it will provide a good black finish if finally polished with a clean linen cloth. White marble can be cleaned with a strong soda water solution (washing soda in water, not drinking soda!) to which quick lime has been added. Leave a thick coat on the marble for a day or two and, after washing it off, finish with a white wax polish. Gold leafed engraved decoration on the marble can be restored after degreasing by buying some goldleaf writing foil from an art shop. Place a sheet over the grooves and run a pointed stick, such as an orange stick, over the foil and in the grooves.

Sometimes a Victorian bracket clock will have been blackened with paint over the gilt ornaments, following a fashion of the past. The ornaments must be removed and treated with paint stripper. If the gilding has gone, the parts can be electro-gilded by a commercial firm.

After a clock movement has been cleaned, it must be oiled with proper clock oil. It is not likely to be oiled again for a long time, human nature being what it is, and clock oil is specially blended to stay oily for several years. Ordinary oils become gummy or dry out much more quickly, causing the clock to stop or increasing wear. Failing clock oil, use sewing machine oil, which also lasts well. Clock oil should always be used for small and precision clocks. Always keep a bottle of clock oil in the dark: light causes it to deteriorate.

When oiling a clock movement, the following rules should be strictly adhered to:
1 Oil only the steel pivots that run in holes in the brass plates (or iron plates in some old clocks). There should be only sufficient oil to fill the clearance in the bearing and partly fill the cup around it (called the 'oil sink') if there is one. The oil should not be enough to run across the clock plate. That will cause oil to be drawn away from the bearing. Over-oiling is all too common.
2 Do NOT oil the wheel teeth, or pinion leaves. They are, for technical reasons, intended to run dry in a clock.
3 There is one exception to the rule above. A trace of oil should be applied to the teeth of the escape wheel—the wheel that is allowed to move in jumps by the

action of the escapement. In a pendulum clock it is the top wheel (usually) with pointed teeth (usually), directly controlled by the swing of the pendulum. It is only necessary to put a smear of oil on two or three teeth. The escapement will distribute it.
4 Put a smear of oil where there is a pin that lifts a lever or where two parts rub together (except teeth).

Now to setting up the clock: as a longcase clock needs more attention in setting up than most, it will be used as the model. The trunk must stand on a firm base against a wall or in a corner. If the clock is not supported, it will not perform well, will tend to stop, and could even be knocked over. The case is best anchored to the wall because any tendency to rock and even loose joints in the case will bring the pendulum to a stop, usually when the weights drop to the length of the pendulum. In the back of the trunk there will usually be some holes where the clock was fastened in the past. A screw through such a hole into a fixing plug in the wall is ideal. If drilling the wall is not possible, place thin wedges under the front of the clock plinth so that the trunk is pressed firmly against the wall. A clock in a corner may be similarly held. Wedges can be made from the halves of a spring clothes peg, suitably shortened.

Next place the seatboard and movement in place and try the hood in position to make sure the dial is centred in the opening. After any necessary adjustment, attach the pendulum and then the weights, seeing that the lines are not tangled. If they have been left in the wound position, round the barrels, they may have become crossed but will run in the grooves on the next winding. Check to see if the pendulum swings truly. If it twists, the suspension spring has become buckled or kinked and a new one will have to be fitted.

The next step is most important for all pendulum clocks: setting the clock in beat. When a clock is in beat there are exactly equal intervals between ticks and tocks. A clock not in beat is liable to stop. With a grandfather or longcase clock that has a seconds hand, the recoil of the hand can be seen. It should be the same at each jump. The clockmaker's method of checking is to move the pendulum to the left until the clock just ticks and then release it. If the clock stops, it is out of beat. Then he does the same in the other direction.

It is common to see clocks propped or wedged at an angle to set them in beat and so keep them going. The correct method is to bend the crutch enough to adjust the clock to the position in which it is standing. Most clocks with pendulums are liable to be placed where they are out of beat, such as on a sloping mantel shelf. If the tick is uneven, lift one side or other of the clock very gently until it is even, which will indicate which way it is out of beat. The crutch has to be bent in that direction. Although crutches are made to be bent, the bending has to be carried out with care otherwise the fork or loop through which the pendulum passes may be broken or twisted, or the pivot of the escapement bent.

Some clocks have automatic beat correction. They include French Brocot clocks and some German ones. The Brocot clocks are those with visible escapements in marble cases. The crutch has a friction joint in it, which will adjust itself to the angle of the clock. Very well made clocks, including almost all regulators, have beat adjustment. On each side of the crutch is an accessible adjusting screw to alter its position in relation to the pendulum.

If the hours struck by a striking clock do not agree with the time shown by the hands, control will be by count wheel, also called 'locking plate.' The count wheel, with a slotted edge, is on the back plate of most French clocks and earlier English ones, but between the plates on many longcase clocks. To set the striking in phase, with a pencil lift the locking lever, an L-shaped arm that drops on the edge of the count wheel. Let it fall again and the clock will strike the next hour or half hour. Continue until the hour is correct for the hands. The minute hand should be at least a quarter of an hour from the striking position when this adjustment is made.

Clocks with rack striking cannot become out of phase unless wrongly assembled or if a hand becomes loose.

Many members of the public can repeat the rule, 'You must never turn the hands of a clock backwards.' If it is a timepiece without strike or chime, no harm is done. The danger is that the snail (a stepped cam of snail-shape in rack-striking clocks) may be damaged. Many later clocks have an overriding device to prevent damage. In a precision clock the escapement may be harmed, although it is a timekeeper only. So, to be on the safe side, with an unknown clock keep to the old rule.

If a clock does not strike on the hour, it may have been assembled incorrectly. If it is a quarter of an hour out, the minute hand probably fits on a square and needs to be removed and turned through 90°. Most clocks have the hour hand held by friction. If it does not point exactly to the hour when it should, it may be possible to move it by gentle pressure, pulling it forward a little first to free it. Too much pressure will snap it off.

A bracket clock or heavy mantle clock that has stopped because it was not wound need not be turned or removed to open the back or side door to set the pendulum swinging. Just lift one side of the clock gently after winding. Let it down again and off will go the clock.

A final point: most clocks run for about thirty hours and are intended to be wound daily, or for eight days and are intended to be wound weekly. Do not wind a clock weekly and then discover after you have had it for ten years that it is a month clock! French clocks were occasionally made to run for two weeks; few owners probably know it.

Bibliography

Some of the books listed below are out of print, but may be borrowed from libraries. The list is not exhaustive because books on horology have been written since the 13th century. In any case, only books in English are included. Thorough study of them, however, combined with practical experience, will certainly translate the reader to the class of the expert.

Finally, a suggestion: anyone who becomes seriously interested in clocks should join the Antiquarian Horological Society, 28 Welbeck Street, London W1M 7PG, or the National Association of Watch and Clock Collectors Inc., P.O. Box 33, Columbia (Pa.), 17512, U.S.A., or both.

Early historical

Edwardes, Ernest L., *Weight-driven Clocks of the Middle Ages and Renaissance*, Altrincham (Cheshire), 1965.

Gordon, G. F. C., *Clockmaking Past and Present*, London, 1946.

Leopold, J. H., *The Amanus Manuscript*, London, 1971.

Robertson, J. Drummond, *The Evolution of Clockwork*, 1931, reprinted Wakefield (Yorkshire) 1972.

Tait, Hugh, *Clocks in the British Museum*, London, 1968.

General historical

Baillie, G. H., C. Clutton and C. A. Ilbert, *Britten's Old Clocks and Watches and their Makers*, London, 1956.

Bruton, Eric, *Clocks and Watches 1400–1900*, London and New York, 1967.

Bruton, Eric, *Clocks and Watches*, London, 1968.

Chamberlain, Paul M., *It's About Time*, New York, 1941.

Jordan, E. V. B., and H. von Bertele, *The Book of Old Clocks and Watches*, English ed. London, 1964.

Lloyd, H. Alan, *Old Clocks*, London, 1958.

Ullyett, Kenneth, *In Quest of Clocks*, London, 1950.

Historical, mainly pictorial

Guye, Samuel, and Henri Michel, *Time and Space, Measuring Instruments from the 15th to the 19th Century*, English ed. London, 1971.

Pippa, Luigi, *Masterpieces of Watchmaking*, Lausanne (Switzerland), 1966. (Actually half is about clocks. Captions in English, French and German.)

Specific types of clock

Bruton, Eric, *The Longcase Clock*, London and New York, 1964.

Coole, P. G., and E. Neumann, *The Orpheus Clocks*, London, 1972.

Edwardes, Ernest L., *The Grandfather Clock*, Altrincham (Cheshire), 1952.

Gould, Lt Cdr Rupert, *The Marine Chronometer*, 1923, reprinted London, 1960.

Hope-Jones, F., *Electrical Timekeeping*, London, 1949.

Royer-Collard, F. B., *Skeleton Clocks*, London, 1969.

National clocks

Bird, Anthony, *English House Clocks 1600–1850*, Newton Abbot (Devon), 1973.

Ceszinski, Herbert, and Malcolm R. Webster, *English Domestic Clocks*, 1913, reprinted London, 1969.

Mody, N. H. N., *Japanese Clocks*, London, 1932.

Palmer, Brooks, *A Treasury of American Clocks*, New York, 1967.

Tyler, E. J., *European Clocks*, London, 1968.

Makers

Lee, R. A., *The Knibb Family, Clockmakers*, Byfleet (Surrey), 1964.

Mussey, Barrows, *Young Father Time*, Downingtown (Pennsylvania), 1950. (About Eli Terry.)

Pioneers of Precision Timekeeping, London, 1965.

Quill, Humphrey, *John Harrison: The Man who found Longitude*, London, 1966.

Roberts, Kenneth D., *The Contributions of Joseph Ives to Connecticut Clock Technology*, Bristol (Connecticut), 1970.

Salomons, Sir David, *Breguet 1747–1823*, London, 1923.

Symonds, R. W., *Thomas Tompion: His Life and Work*, London, 1951.

Willard, John Ware, *Simon Willard and his Clocks*, New York, 1962.

Reference books

Baillie, G. H., *Clocks and Watches – An Historical Bibliography*, London, 1951.

Baillie, G. H., *Watchmakers and Clockmakers of the World*, London, 1970.

Bruton, Eric, *Dictionary of Clocks and Watches*, London and New York, 1962.

Carle, Donald De, *Watch and Clock Encyclopedia*, London, 1959.

Carle, Donald De, *Clocks and their Value*, London, 1971.

Ward, F. A. B., *Time Measurement* (catalogue of the Science Museum, London, collection, with historical notes).

Practical books

Carle, Donald De, *Practical Clock Repairing*, London, 1971.

Gazeley, W. J., *Clock and Watch Escapements*, London, 1973.

Player, J. W. (ed.), *Britten's Watch and Clock Makers' Handbook, Dictionary and Guide*, London, 1955.

Miscellaneous

Cumhail, P. G., *Investing in Clocks and Watches*, London, 1967.

Lloyd, H. Alan, *Some Outstanding Clocks over Seven Hundred Years, 1250–1950*, London, 1958.

Rawlings, A. L., *The Science of Clocks and Watches*, London, n.d.

Periodicals with at least some antiquarian interest

American Horologist and Jeweler, Denver (Colorado).

Antiquarian Horology, London. (All antiquarian.)

Bulletin of the National Association of Watch and Clock Collectors, Columbia (Pennsylvania). (All antiquarian.)

Horological Journal, Ashford (Kent).

Swiss Watch and Jewelry Journal, English ed. Lausanne (Switzerland).

Index

The numbers in bold type refer to
illustrations

Act of Parliament clocks 53, **58**
alarms 78, 87, **16, 22, 48, 74, 77, 79, 90**
anchor escapement 38, 45, 51, 53, 62,
    66, 70, 79, **1, 21, 32, 44, 48, 50, 83**
animated clocks 86
anniversary clocks 86
antiques fairs 13
arbor 18, 27, 29, 31, 38, 76, **61**
Arnold, John 57
Arts et Métiers Museum, Paris 68
auctions 13, 14, 27, 28
automata 16, 17, 27, 78, 86, **49, 78**

Baillie, G. H. 15, 16
Bain clock 87
balance 24, 25, 66, 84, **21, 81**
balloon clocks 51, 65, **52**
banjo clocks 79, **85**
Barlow, Edward 45, **37**
Barnard, J. 53
Barraud & Lund 53
beam engine clock **93**
bedpost construction 21
beechwood 76
Berthoud, Ferdinand 68
bezel 44
Big Ben 22, 49, **75**
birdcage construction 21
bob 34, 53, 86
bob pendulum 44, 45, **42, 43, 47**
bolt and shutter maintaining power 31
Boulle 65, **34, 52, 68**
Bovet family 64
bracket clocks 9, 31, 36, 38, 43, 44, 45,
    49, 51, 60, 62, 66, 86, 90, 92, 93, **41,
    42, 43, 44, 45, 46, 49, 51, 59, 62**
break-arch 44, 51, 62, 70, 76, 78, **18,
    45, 46, 48**
Breguet, Abraham-Louis 9, 67, 68, **50**
'British Clockmaker's Heritage, The',
    exhibition 16
British Horological Institute 15, 16
Britten, F. J. 15, 16
Brocot clocks 82, 93, **76, 87**
Bulle electric clock 87
Burgess, Martin 10

Cambridge chimes 49
carriage clocks 11, 67, 82. 84, 90, 91,
    79, 90, 91
cartel clocks 66
Cassiobury Park clock 21, **14**
Cescinsky, Herbert 15
Ceulen, Johannes van **28**
chamber clock **30**
chapter ring 39, 43, 44, 60, 66, 91
Charles I 15
Chelsea Antiques Fair 21
Chesne, Claudius Du **41**
chiming mechanisms 49, **54, 59**
chiming train 18, 31
Christie's, London 13
chronometer clocks 10
circular error 34, 38
Clement, William 38, **32**
clock glasses 11
Clockmakers' Company *see* Worshipful
    Company of Clockmakers
clock oil 92
Clocks in the British Museum (Tait) 16
Clowes, James 33
Clutton, C. 16
coaching clocks 11, 53, 57
Comtoise clocks 70
Congreve rolling ball clocks 10, **5**
contrate wheel 27, 34, 36, 70
Coole, Philip 16
Coster, Salomon 34, 60, **28**
cottage clocks 43
count wheel 28, 29, 93, **11**
Courvoisier & Compe **89**
cow's tail pendulum **77**
craft guilds 14, 15
Cromwell, Oliver 7
cross-beat escapements 14
crown wheel 24, 25, 29, 34, 36, 38, 60,
    70, **42, 61**
crutch 34, 90, 91, 92, 93, **11**
cuckoo clocks 76
Cumhail, P. G. 16
cycloidal cheeks 34

dead-beat escapement 66
deal 43
Dent, William **39**
Dent & Co. **5, 75**
Dent, Barraud & Sons 53
dials 10, 27, 36, 38, 39, 40, 43, 44, 53,
    57, 60, 62, 66, 67, 76, 91, **15, 17, 18,
    22, 24, 25, 27, 29, 30, 40, 41, 45, 46,
    56, 57, 62, 66**
digital clocks 86, **94**
Directoire period 68, **69**
dolphin fret **20**
domestic clocks 24, 25, 28, 34, 38, 91,
    93
Dondi, Giovanni de **4**
driving wheels 18
drum movements 66

Earnshaw, Thomas 57
East, Edward **44**
ebony 43
Edgar, Gilbert 16
Edwardes, E. L. 16
Eglomi 11
8-day clocks 41, 43, **32, 37**
electric clocks 87
electrotyping 10, 27
Ellicott, John 45
Empire period 10, 68, 70
English dials 57, 60
English Domestic Clocks (Cescinsky and
    Webster) 15
escapement 14, 18, 24, 25, 29, 34, 38,
    44, 66, 82, 84, 85, 90, 93, **16, 43, 49,
    61, 63, 73, 76, 81**; *see also* anchor,
    dead-beat, pin-wheel, platform, verge
    escapements
escape wheel 18, 38, 79, 84, 92
Eureka clock 87
Evelyn, John 7
Exeter cathedral clock 21

'Fanatics, The' 7
fishtail piercing 45, 51
flatbed frame 22

flat top clocks 51
flute clocks 49
fly **42**
flying pendulum clocks 86
foliot 22, 24, 25, 34, 60, 76, **16, 17, 23,
    70**
*Former Clock and Watchmakers and
    Their Work* (Britten) 15
French, J. M. **50**
French Revolution 67
400-day clocks 86, 87
Fromanteel, Ahasuerus 34
furnishing clocks 13
fusee 27, 29, 31, 53, 57, 66, 82, **19, 23,
    42, 71, 75, 88, 89**

Galerie am Neumarkt, Geneva 13
Gille L'Ainé **65**
girandole clocks 79
glass paintings 11
going barrel 31, 66
going train 18, 41, **27**
Gothic clocks 24, 25, 28, **17**
Gould, Christopher 38
Graham, George 53, 66, **36, 60**
grande sonnerie 84, **89**
Grandfather Clock, The (Edwardes) 16
grandfather clocks 9, 92
great wheel 29
Greenwich Observatory 57
Gretton **3**
Grosvenor House Antiques Fair, London
    13
Gunning, John 87

Haage klokje 60
Haley, Thomas 13
'Halifax Moon' dial **37**
Handley & Moore **48**
hands 40, 43, 57, 85, 86
hanging ball clocks 10
Harrison, John and James 11, 53, 57,
    68, **72**
Hill Bros **54**
Hipp clock 87
hoods 38, 62, 90, **35**
Hooke, Robert 38
Horological Journal, The 15
horological sculptures 10
Huygens, Christiaan 34, 45, 60, **28, 63**
Hyde, T. & S. **6**

Ilbert, Courtenay A. 16, **10**
Industrial Revolution 7, 8, 9, 10, 70, 82,
    84, 87
Investing in Clocks and Watches
    (Cumhail) 16
iron clocks 21, 22, 24, 25, 28, **14, 15, 16,
    17**

jack 17, 27
'Jack Blandifer' 17
Jackson, Stops & Staff, London 13
Jacob the Zech **23**
Jacomart 17
Janvier, Antide 68
Japy Frères **90**
Jenkins, Henry **13**
Junghaus, Erhardt 78

Kaendler, J. J. **65**
Ketterer, Anton 76
kingwood 44
Knibb, Joseph 38, **31**
Knibb Family, Clockmakers, The (Lee) 16

lacquer decoration 39, 44
lancet shape 51
lantern clocks 24, 25, 28, 29, 36, 41, 43,
    18, 20, 21
leaves 18
Lee, R. A. 16
lenticular pendulum 45, 51, 53, **51**
Leonardo da Vinci 16, 29
Lepaute, Jean André 68
Le Roy, Pierre 68
lighthouse clocks 84, **92**
Lloyd, H. A. 16
locking plate *see* count wheel
longcase clocks 10, 15, 18, 31, 34, 36,
    38, 39, 40, 41, 43, 44, 52, 60, 62, 66,
    67, 70, 79, 90, 92, 93, **6, 11, 31, 32,
    33, 37, 39, 68**
Louis XIV period 62, **68**
Louis XV period 65, 66
lyre-shaped clock 66, 79

mahogany 39, 51, 53, 86, **40, 43, 48, 54,
    56, 59**
mainspring 18, 27, 29
mantel clocks 14, 51, 82, 93, **65, 75**
marble clocks 92, **74**
marine chronometer 10, 57, 91, **8, 56**
marquetry 39, 44, **33**
Marton & Gain S. A. **7**
Masson, Denis 67
Meissen **65**
memorandum clock 82
Mercer, Thomas **8**
mercury pendulums 91
mock pendulum 45, 62, **41, 45**
module 66
Montgolfier brothers 65
Moon dials 40, 43, 62, **40**
Morbier clocks 70
musical clocks 49, **49**
mystery clocks 85

Nardin, Ulysse **8**
Neuchâteloise clock 65
novelty clocks 27, 28

oak 39, 43, 52, 65, 82, **37**
ogee (OG) clocks 79
oil sink 92
Old Clocks (Lloyd) 16
*Old Clocks and Watches and their
    Makers* (Britten) 15
*Old English Master Clockmakers and
    their Clocks, The* (Cescinsky) 15
olive wood 39, 44
'one at the hour' clock 82
organ clocks 49, **78**
ormolu clocks 10, 67, 68, 70, **49, 52, 57,
    67, 74**
Orpheus clocks 28, **29**

pagoda top clocks 51

pallets 25, 38
Parkinson & Frodsham, London **56**
parquetry 39
Payne, London **71**
Pearson, Page & Jewsbury, Birmingham **9**
pearwood 65
pendule d'officier **79**, **89**
Pendule Française, La (Tardy) 15, 16
pendulum 9, 18, 25, 31, 34, 36, 38, 43, 44, 45, 53, 57, 60, 62, 66, 68, 70, 78, 79, 82, 85, 86, 87, 90, 92, 93, **18**, **21**, **25**, **28**, **30**, **38**, **42**, **43**, **58**, **61**, **62**, **63**, **70**, **72**, **73**, **76**, **77**, **81**, **88**
Pepys, Samuel 7
piercing, decorative 45, **67**
pigeon clocks 11
pillar clock 66
pillars 17, 38
pinions 18, 36
pin wheel escapement 66
pivot holes 91, **12**
pivots 18, 34
Plantart, N. **27**
plate frame clocks 27, **61**
platform escapement 84
Polygraphice (Salmon) 10
post chaise clocks 57
posted frame movements 27, 41, 43, 60, 62
postman's alarm clock 78

Quare, Daniel **34**, **46**, **47**

rack gravity clocks 10
rack striking 45, 93, **44**
railway clocks 11
railway engine clocks 84

Raingo, M. 68
Regency clocks 53, 68
Register of Apprentices 15
regulators 10, 53, 66, 67, 86, 90, 9 3, 3 5, **60**
religieuse clock 62
repeaters 45, 49, 57, 84, **74**, **89**, 90
reproduction clocks 9, 10
rising hoods 90
Road Traffic Act (1934) 87
Rogers, Isaac 18
rolling ball clocks 10, **5**
rosewood **50**
Rye church clock 21

Salisbury cathedral clock 21
Salmon, William 10
seatboard 43
Second Empire period 10, 70
seconds hand 38, 92
security clocks 11
sedan clocks 57
'shake' 53
shelf clocks 9, 10, 60, 79, 82
skeleton clocks 10, 82, 91, **55**, **88**
skeletonised clocks 68
Smith, J. 53, **55**
snail 93
Sotheby's, London 13
Sotheby's Parke Bernet Inc., New York 13
spandrels 39, 43, 44, **49**
spring-driven clocks 24, 25, 27, 28, 29, 31, 34, 36, 38, 43, 53, 57, 66, 76, 84, 90, 91, **19**, **22**
stackfreed 29
staartklok 62
staff 24, 36, 38
star wheel 29

steeple shelf clock 79
stoelklok 60, 62
stopwork 29
Story, William **49**
Stripling, Thomas **35**
striking clocks 45, 76, 93, **32**, **50**, **54**, **69**
striking train 18, 29, 31, 41, **27**
sundial **36**
suspension spring 90, 92, **92**, **93**
Symonds, R. W. 16

tabernacle clocks 27, **19**, **25**
table clocks 27, 28, 34, 36, 51, 62, **22**, **26**, **27**, **29**
Tait, Hugh 16
tavern clocks 53, **58**
Telleruhr **61**
Terry, Eli 11, 79
30-hour clocks 41, 43, **39**
Thomas, Seth 79, **83**
Thomas Tompion, His Life and Work (Symonds) 16
Thwaites & Reed, London 15, **4**, **51**
ticket clocks 86, **94**
tidal dials 40
Tiffany Never-wind electric clock 87
Time Measurement (Ward) 16
time recorders 9, 87
time switches 9, 87
Tompion, Thomas 45, 53, 66, 86, **1**, **2**, **11**, **95**
torsion pendulum 86, 87, **92**
tortoise clocks 85
tortoiseshell 44, 65, **34**, **49**, **52**, **68**
Trade Descriptions Act (1968) 14
Trading Standards Department 14
train 18, 29, 31
travelling clocks 11
trumpeter clock **80**

turret clocks 21, 22, 25, 34, 60, **63**

Udall, Thomas **53**
ultrasonic cleaners 91

vase clock 67, **64**
verge, verge escapement 24, 25, 29, 34, 36, 38, 44, 45, 60, 70, 76, 90, **18**, **21**, **27**, **39**, **42**, **43**, **49**, **61**, **81**, **89**
Vernis, Martin 65, 66
verres eglomisés 11, **82**
Vienna regulator 86

Walker, Thomas **40**
wall clocks 9, 21, 36, 53, 57, 60, 62, 78, 86, **77**,
walnut 39, 44, 53, **31**
Ward, Dr F. A. B. 16
warning 29
Watch and Clockmaker's Handbook (Britten) 16
Watchmakers and Clockmakers of the World (Baillie) 15
watchmen's clocks 11, 87
water clocks 15, **9**
Webster, Malcolm R. 15
weight-driven clocks 18, 24, 25, 28, 31, 34, 43, 60, 76, 78, 79, 90, **58**, **62**
Wells cathedral clock 21
Westminster chimes 49, **54**, **59**
Wimbourne minster clock 21
winding square 18
wooden clocks 11
Worshipful Company of Clockmakers, London 15, 16, 53

Acknowledgments

It is often difficult to thank people connected with horology adequately for their help because, with only a few exceptions, they are very generous with their knowledge and time. Even in company like this, Beresford Hutchinson of the British Museum is outstanding for his patience, for the trouble he takes in solving problems and for the almost diffident way in which he will correct one's wrong thinking. I want to thank him particularly for his helpful suggestions made when reading the proofs of this book.

The Trustees of the British Museum and three dealers with workshops (The Clock Shop at Weybridge, Surrey; Aubrey Brocklehurst, of Cromwell Road, West London; and Kingston Antiques of Kingston-upon-Thames) have been especially cooperative in providing facilities for photography, despite the inconvenience to themselves, and I would like to record my grateful thanks to them.

Pictures have come from many sources but particularly the great London auction rooms, Sotheby & Co. and Christie, Manson & Woods, who have been most generous with prints. Without them I could not have hoped to fill the various chronological gaps.

In detail, especial thanks are due to the following:

For allowing me to take my own photographs: The Trustees of the British Museum, London 15, 16, 20, 21, 25, 26, 36, 41, 46, 47, 61, 64, 70; The Clock Shop, Weybridge, Surrey 13, 30, 52, 53, 57, 71, 75, 76, 79; Mr W. F. L. Salloway, of Lichfield, Staffordshire 35.
For facilities for photography: Aubrey Brocklehurst, Cromwell Road, London SW7 83, 84; Kingston Antiques, Kingston-upon-Thames, Surrey 85. Photography by Hawkley Studios Associates.
For the use of photographs: Jürgen Abeler, Wuppertal-Elberfeld, W. Germany 68; Biggs of Maidenhead, Twyford, Berkshire 73, 74; Christie, Manson & Woods, London 44, 49, 67, 77, 78, 81, 89; Christie, Manson & Woods, Geneva 65; Ernest L. Edwardes, Sale, Cheshire 18; Mr C. L. Goggs 39; W. R. Harvey and Co. (Antiques) Ltd, London 40; Kingston Antiques, Kingston-upon-Thames, Surrey 32; Phillips of Hitchin, Hertfordshire 48; A. Podd & Son, Dunstable, Bedfordshire 69; Science Museum, London 62; The Society of Antiquaries, London 23; Sotheby's Belgravia, London 50, 54, 59, 86, 87, 90, 91, 92.

94, 95 are from the Hamlyn Group Picture Library, photographs by Edward Leigh.